COMPUTER STUDIES

GCSE Grade Booster

Halina J. Kasperowicz

Schofield & Sims Ltd.

0 7217 4621 7

First printed 1992

Acknowledgement
The author and the publishers would like to thank the Halifax Building Society for their permission to reproduce the photograph on page 57.

Schofield & Sims Ltd.
Dogley Mill
Fenay Bridge
Huddersfield
HD8 0NQ
England

Typeset by Ocean, Leeds

Printed in Great Britain by the Alden Press, Oxford

Contents

Introduction

Grade Boosters are a series of books which have been produced to enable students to improve their grade in the GCSE examinations. In the GCSE, there has been a move away from factual knowledge to a more practical approach of active learning. However, knowledge of the subject is still vital, both in order to perform the practical aspects of the course and also to answer the Question Papers which test factual knowledge and the ability to apply that knowledge to relevant situations.

The Computer Studies Grade Booster has been written in an attempt to present, in a concise form, the facts required for the GCSE Computer Studies examination. It is intended purely as a revision aid – *not* as a comprehensive text book.

1 Computers and their Main Components

What is a Computer? A computer is a special machine that can be instructed to take in, sort, compare and process information, and output the results in a useful way.

Computers always use some sort of electronic memory to do this.

A computer can make calculations far quicker than a human brain but it needs to be told what to do and to be given all the facts it requires. Computers cannot think for themselves. They can only follow instructions.

Flow of Information through a Computer

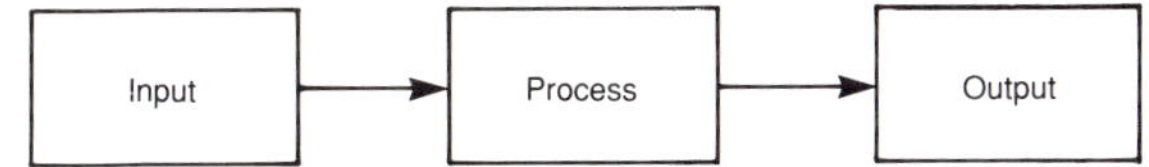

Hardware and Software Computers can be said to be made up of *hardware* and *software*.

Hardware The hardware is all the physical devices which are found in a computer system.

Software The software is all the *programs* (instructions) which are required to make use of the computer.

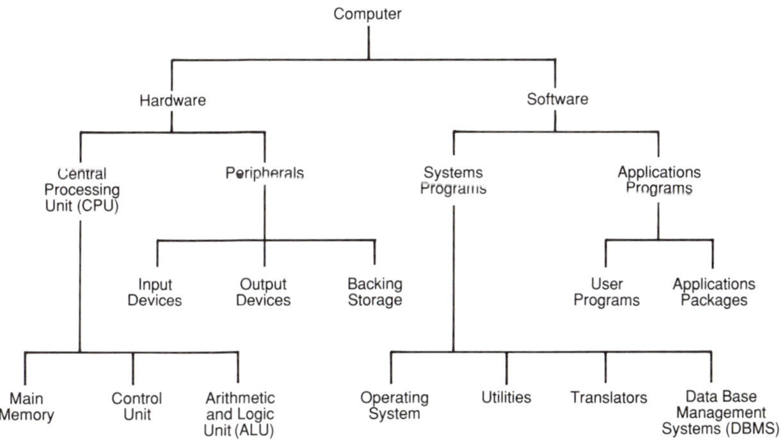

The Main Components of a Computer

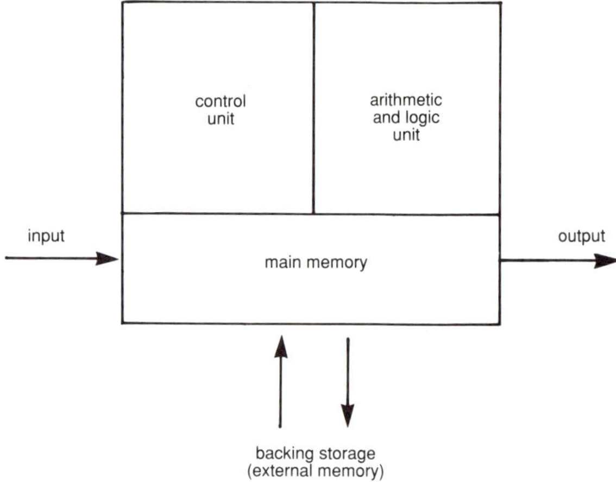

Central Processing Unit (CPU)

Processing takes place in the *central processing unit* (CPU).

The CPU is made up of three main parts:

- the *Control Unit*;
- the *Arithmetic and Logic Unit* (ALU);
- *Main Memory* – also known as Immediate Access Store (IAS), Internal Memory.

The CPU has a number of *registers* (special storage locations) which store the particular data and the instructions which the computer is working with at the time. The most important registers are:

- the *Program Counter* (Sequence Control Register);
- the *Instruction Register*;
- the *Accumulator*.

Program Counter

The program counter (or sequence control register) holds the address (the location in the memory store) of the instruction the program is carrying out. It 'keeps' the computer's place in the program.

Instruction Register

The instruction register holds the actual program instruction the computer is carrying out at the time.

Accumulator

The accumulator holds the item of data that is being processed at the time. After a processing operation has been performed, the accumulator then holds the result of that operation.

Control Unit The control unit co-ordinates the step-by-step running of the whole computer, and regulates the flow of data and instructions to and from the main memory, during input and output, to and from backing store, and within the CPU itself. The control unit is responsible also for the timing of all the operations performed by the computer.

The control unit operates by dealing with each instruction in turn in an operation called the *fetch-execute* cycle, which is repeated millions of times per second.

Fetch-execute Cycle The control unit 'fetches' the requisite instruction from main memory. The program counter locates the instruction, which is copied into the instruction register. Then it 'executes' (carries out) the instruction. Most instructions refer to a data item in memory, or the one in the accumulator. The result is usually placed in the accumulator.

The contents of the program counter are then adjusted, so that it holds the address of the next instruction.

Arithmetic and Logic Unit (ALU) The ALU has two functions:

- it carries out arithmetic, e.g. addition and subtraction;
- it performs certain 'logical' operations, e.g. testing whether two data items match.

Main Memory Main memory, main storage, immediate access store, internal memory are all names for the internal storage of a computer, which holds the program instructions and the data that is being processed. It will also store the intermediate results of any processing awaiting transfer to the output devices.

Registers The main memory consists of a large number of storage locations called *registers*. Each register contains a *byte* (8 bits) or a *word* (12, 16, 24, 32 or 48 bits). Each register is located by means of an address.

Integrated Circuits The main memory is made up from solid state (i.e. without any moving parts) semi-conductor memory circuits called *integrated circuits* or 'chips'.

These are of two types:

- *RAM (Random Access Memory)*
- *ROM (Read Only Memory).*

RAM (Random Access Memory) RAM is the read/write memory which allows any memory call to be accessed immediately, and allows data to be written to it. It forms most of the main memory and is used to store data and programs temporarily. RAM is constantly being re-used for different data items or programs as required.

RAM is *volatile*, i.e. data is lost when the power is switched off.

ROM (Read Only Memory) ROM stores data and instructions permanently and cannot be altered. ROM is *non-volatile*, i.e. its contents are permanently set when the computer is made and the stored information is not lost when the power is switched off.

ROM forms a small part of the main storage. It is used to store initial data and those programs that need to be in storage at all times, such as the boot program (see page 65) which is needed to get the computer going when it is switched on, or the patterns of dots needed to form characters on the screen. Other programs can be held in backing storage and loaded into RAM as and when they are required.)

Bus A *bus* is a set of lines along which signals travel from one part of the CPU to another.

Address Bus An *address bus* is a set of lines on which an address can be sent from one part of the computer to another.

Data Bus A *data bus* is a set of lines used to transfer data from one part of a computer to another.

Control Line A *control line* is a line along which the signals travel that control parts of the computer.

Parallel and Serial Transmission Within the computer, signals travel in *parallel*, i.e. several electrical signals move round the computer together on separate tracks. In most electrical equipment, e.g. printers, cassette recorders, the signals travel in *series*, i.e. one after the other along a single track.

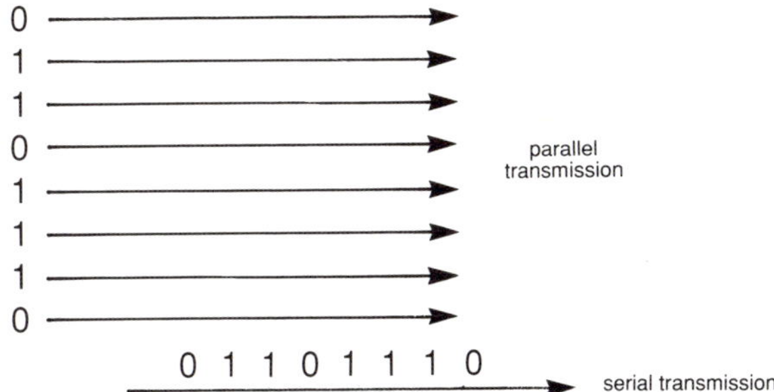

Peripheral A *peripheral* is any device outside the computer's central processing unit but under its control. Input devices, output devices and backing storage devices are all peripherals.

Types of Computer Computers fall into three categories:

- *Mainframe* computers;
- *Minicomputers*;
- *Microcomputers*.

Mainframe Computers Mainframes are large, powerful and expensive computers with a range of powerful input/output, processing and storage facilities.

Minicomputers (Minis) Minicomputers are smaller, less expensive versions of mainframe computers. The dividing line between the two is blurred.

Microcomputers Microcomputers are small, cheap, multi-purpose computers. A microcomputer's CPU is a *microprocessor*, which is an integrated circuit containing the control unit, arithmetic and logic unit and usually some memory. Modern large-scale integration (LSI) technology has allowed all these components to fit on to a single chip.

Microcomputers can be sub-divided into three categories:

- Business micros;
- Home computers;
- Portable micros.

Business Micros Business micros are usually known as *personal computers* (PCs) and are useful for routine business work such as word processing, data management and spreadsheets. PCs can be linked into larger computer networks.

Home Computers Home computers are usually cheaper than business micros. They tend to be *stand-alone* machines, i.e. they are not linked with other computers. Games software and colour graphics are their strong selling points. Backing storage is usually in the form of cassette tapes, floppy disks or cartridges.

Portable Micros Portable micros are small and light enough to carry around. They can be divided into *luggables* which are fairly heavy and *laptops* which are the size of a briefcase and truly portable. They have been designed for taking to meetings when the person needing them is travelling by car or by air.

Microcomputer Systems in a Small Business A typical microcomputer system in a small business consists of:

A microcomputer;
disk drives;
hard and floppy disks to store programs and data;
a printer;
and sometimes a *modem* (acoustic coupler, see page 53) to link with other computers via the telephone network.

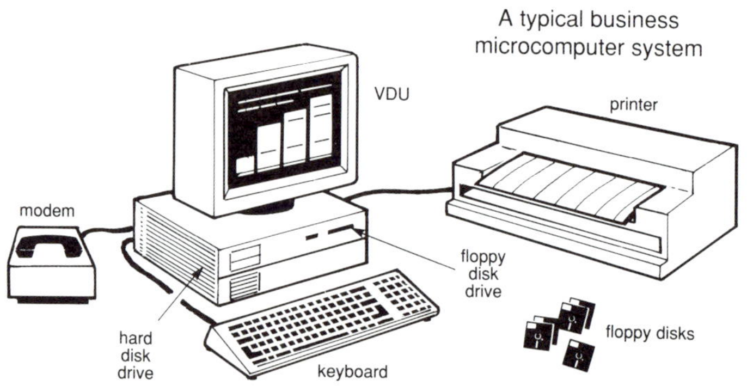

A typical business microcomputer system

Applications Programs in a Small Business Typical applications programs used in a small business are:

- *Accounting programs* which cover payroll, ledger, sales, purchasing, invoicing.
- *Financial modelling* with the use of spreadsheet packages for budgetary forecasting and control.
- *Word processing* with the production of business correspondence, especially standard letters.
- *Data management* which allows the keeping of up-to-date files on the computer, with facilities to update, amend, insert and delete.

Analogue Computers Analogue computers represent data in a *continuous* manner and are best suited for use with quantities that vary with time, such as temperature and pressure. They are used in scientific and engineering procedures, especially *process control* (see page 13).

Real Time An analogue computer works in *real time*. This means that values are output and displayed as they are calculated, without any delay.

Generally, an analogue computer cannot store any values.

The output from an analogue computer is usually:

a moving display, e.g. a line on an oscilloscope screen;
a drawn line, e.g. on a graph plotter;
an electrical signal which can be used to control another device, such as on the production line of a car plant.

The accuracy of an analogue computer is limited by its components and by the precision with which input starting values can be set and output values can be read.

Digital Computers Digital computers represent data in a *discrete* manner. Numbers are represented by 'pulses' of electricity. Such computers are used to perform mathematical calculations and are the type used in commercial data processing.

Analogue-to-Digital Converter (ADC) Often a digital computer is required to accept input from an analogue device. An analogue-to-digital converter is needed to change the analogue signal to a digital one. The converter consists of an integrated circuit which takes in a voltage in a given range and sends this out as a set of two-state signals, i.e. it converts it into a set of binary signals.

Digital-to-Analogue Converter (DAC) If a digital computer outputs to an analogue device, then a digital-to-analogue converter is required to convert the digital signal to one of varying voltage.

Hybrid Computers Hybrid computers are a combination of analogue and digital devices linked by an ADC. Hybrids are used for flight simulators, for building design and for military purposes.

Interface An *interface* is the hardware and associated software needed for communication between processors and peripheral devices, to compensate for their different operating characteristics.

Parallel Interface In a computer, all signals are parallel signals and a *parallel interface* is used to connect the computer to a piece of equipment which also works with parallel signals, e.g. to attach a parallel printer to a computer.

Serial Interface A *serial interface* converts the computer's parallel signals into serial signals, which travel one behind the other. It is used to connect a computer (which works in parallel mode) to equipment which works in serial mode, e.g. to attach a serial printer to a computer.

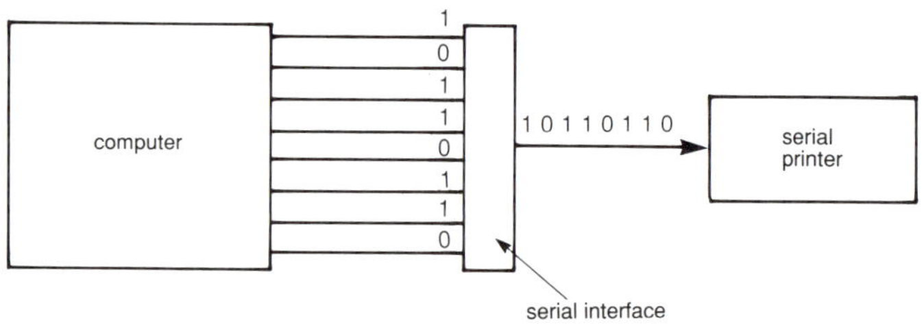

Buffer If two devices that are connected together through an interface work at different speeds, then a store is needed to hold data while one device is waiting for the other. This store is called a *buffer*. In a computer system the CPU works at much higher speeds than the peripherals, e.g. the printers, so that buffers are needed.

Port A *port* is the point at which signals from peripherals enter the central computing system.

Process Control *Process control* is the use of computers (usually analogue or hybrid) to control directly the operation of a physical process, e.g. the automatic control of electrical power generation or chemical plants.

Control Program A *control program* is a set of instructions used to control the operation of a device.

Automatic control systems can have *hard-wired* control using logic circuits (i.e. permanent circuitry which is fixed at manufacture), or be under software program control. Using software control allows a much more flexible system.

The action of a control system is measured by sensors which can detect such things as temperature and humidity and adjust a process accordingly.

Feedback *Feedback* is the term used for the cycle in control systems which aims to keep something at a steady level, e.g. temperature, or travelling in a fixed direction. Responses to change must be as fast as possible, and reliability is essential.

Feedback Cycle

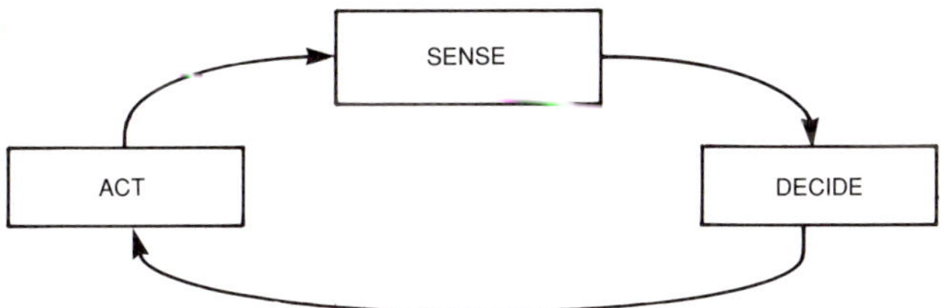

2 Number Systems

Decimal System The normal counting system has ten digits 0, 1, 2, 3, 4, 5, 6, 7, 8, 9. It is called the *decimal* (base-10) or *denary* system.

Place-values are used to indicate numbers higher than 9.

For example, 9643
means that there are 9 thousands
6 hundreds
4 tens
3 ones.

If we put column headings over this number, we would get:

1000	100	10	1
9	6	4	3

In a computer, switches are used to represent numbers. The switch is either *OFF* or *ON*, giving rise to a two-state system.

A switch which is OFF represents a 0, and a switch which is ON represents a 1.

Binary System In order to use this system to do calculations a number system was introduced that uses only the digits 0 and 1. This is called the *binary* (base-2) system.

Binary Digits (bits) The digits 0 and 1 are called *binary digits* or *bits*.

In the binary system, the value of the digits increases in powers of 2 from right to left, so the column headings are as follows:

← and so on 128 64 32 16 8 4 2 1

Using these column headings in the binary system, the decimal number 50 is represented as:

32	16	8	4	2	1
1	1	0	0	1	0

This is calculated as:

$32 + 16 + 2 = 50.$

So 50 in decimal = 110010 in binary.

The Decimal Numbers 0-10 and their Binary Equivalents

Decimal	Binary
0	0
1	1
2	10
3	11
4	100
5	101
6	110
7	111
8	1000
9	1001
10	1010

Addition in Binary Notation

When using decimal numbers we start an addition by first adding the units, then the tens, then the hundreds, etc.

If the numbers in any column add up to ten or more, the number of tens is carried to the next column to the left, i.e. tens of units are carried to the tens column, tens of tens to the hundreds column and so on: e.g.

```
  5 7 6
+   6 6
  1 1
  -----
  6 4 2
```

The process is the same with binary numbers. We first add the numbers in the units column, then the numbers in the two's column, then those in the four's column, and so on. This time, if the numbers in any column add up to two or more, the number of twos is carried to the next column to the left, i.e. twos of units are carried to the two's column, twos of twos are carried to the four's column and so on.

e.g.

```
    0       0       1       1
  + 0     + 1     + 0     + 1
                           1
  ---     ---     ---     ---
    0       1       1     1 0

  11011
 + 1001
 11  11
 ------
 100100
```

Subtraction in Binary Notation

Computers are designed to add two numbers together. Subtraction is done by a clever method using twos complement.

For example, let us look at

101 – 10

1st Step. Make the number of digits the same by adding 0s where needed, i.e. 10 becomes 010.

2nd Step. Find the *twos complement* of the number which is to be taken away (010) by 'flipping' the 1s to 0s and the 0s to 1s, so 010 becomes 101, *then* adding 1 to the units digit.

```
 101
  +1
 ---
 110
 ---
```

so the twos complement of 010 is 110.

3rd Step. Add the twos complement to the other number in the sum

```
   101
 + 110
 -----
  1011
 -----
```

4th Step. Knock off the leftmost 1. This leaves 011, which is the correct answer for the subtraction exercise.

Arithmetic in a Computer

Computers are designed to add two binary numbers at a time. So, if four numbers are to be added, the first two are added together, then the third number is added to this result, and the fourth number is added to that result.

Multiplication

Multiplication is done by adding over and over again. Complex calculations, such as finding the square root of a number, are broken down into steps which involve addition alone.

Division

Division is done by subtracting over and over again (the subtraction itself being broken down into steps which involve addition alone).

Representation of Positive and Negative Numbers

There are two methods of representation:

- *sign and magnitude*;
- *twos complement*.

1. Sign and Magnitude

The leftmost digit is used to indicate the sign:

0 for positive,
1 for negative.

The remaining digits give the number in binary notation:

e.g. 0 0010101 = + 10101
1 0010101 = − 10101

sign digit — number

2. Twos Complement

The leftmost digit indicates the sign:

0 for positive,
1 for negative.

Positive numbers are represented in binary. Negative numbers are represented by their twos complement:

e.g. 0 0000101 = + 101
1 1111011 = − 101

sign digit — number

Binary Fractions

The numbers we have looked at so far have all been *integers* (whole numbers). Real numbers, i.e. those with a fractional part, can also be represented in binary notation. However, not all decimal fractions can be represented exactly and this can lead to errors in calculations.

Place-value column headings for the binary fractions are:

$\frac{1}{2}$	$\frac{1}{4}$	$\frac{1}{8}$	$\frac{1}{16}$	→ and so on

Examples of Decimal Fractions and their Binary Equivalents

Decimal	Binary
0.5	0.1000
0.25	0.0100
0.125	0.0010
0.0625	0.0001

Octal Numbers This is a base-8 number system, using the 8 digits: 0, 1, 2, 3, 4, 5, 6, 7.

Place-value column headings are: 64 8 1.

Using these column headings in the octal system the decimal number 162 is represented as:

64	8	1
2	4	2

This is calculated as: 2 × 64 = 128
4 × 8 = 32
2 × 1 = 2,

so 128 + 32 + 2 = 162,
so 162 in decimal = 242 in octal.

Hexadecimal Numbers This is a base-16 number system. The decimal numbers 10 to 15 have letter substitutes, so the symbols used are:
0, 1, 2, 3, 4, 5, 6, 7, 8, 9, A, B, C, D, E, F.

Place-value column headings are: 256 16 1.

Using these headings in the hexadecimal system, the decimal number 79 is represented as:

256	16	1
	4	F

This is calculated as:

16 × 4 = 64
15 × 1 = 15,
64 + 15 = 79

so 79 in decimal = 4F in hexadecimal.

Use of Octal and Hexadecimal Notation Octal and hexadecimal notation are often used as a shorthand method for representing binary numbers. Binary notation is very confusing to the human eye, and where it is necessary for binary codes to be written or read, e.g. by programmers, the octal and hexadecimal notations can be used. These notations are easier to read and are easily converted to binary:

an *octal* digit represents a group of *three* binary digits, e.g. 6 in octal = 110 in binary;

a *hexadecimal* digit represents a group of *four* binary digits, e.g. D in hexadecimal = 1101 in binary.

Byte *Byte* was originally the term used for the smallest group of bits used to represent one character. It is now used to mean 8 bits.

Kilobytes (K bytes) *Kilo* in the metric system is used for one thousand (1 000). In computing terms it is the nearest number to one thousand in the binary place values and is 2 to the power 10 (2^{10}), which is 1024.

1 Kilobyte = 1024 bytes = 8192 bits.

Megabytes (M bytes) *Mega* in the metric system is used for one million (1 000 000). In computing terms it is the nearest number to one million in the binary place values and is 2 to the power 20 (2^{20}), which is 1 048 576.

1 Megabyte = 1 048 576 bytes.

Gigabytes (G bytes) *Giga* in the metric system is used for one thousand million (1 000 000 000). In computing terms it is the nearest number to one thousand million in the binary place values and is 2 to the power 30 (2^{30}) which is 1 073 741 824.

1 Gigabyte = 1 073 741 824 bytes.

Character Set A *character set* is a group of characters which is accepted as valid by a particular computer. For example, a 64-character machine code might consist of 26 alphabetic characters A to Z, 10 digits 0 to 9, and 28 special characters (including 'space').

Errors in Computer Calculations Errors sometimes occur in computer calculations due to the shortcomings of computer arithmetic. The most common errors are:

loss of accuracy and *overflow*.

Loss of Accuracy Loss of accuracy occurs because of the limited amount of storage space available for each number. (If each number stored is inaccurate, then the results of any arithmetic performed on these numbers can be even more inaccurate.)

If not all the digits of a number can be stored, then the number will be either *truncated* or *rounded*.

Truncation If a number is truncated, the digits which cannot be stored are simply lost.

Truncation errors occur with fractions that cannot be represented exactly as decimals, e.g. $\frac{1}{3}$, $\frac{2}{3}$, or when the result of a division does not give an exact answer.

Rounding If a number is rounded, the last digits which can be stored are adjusted to make the number as accurate as possible.

Rounding is often done to reduce truncation errors.

Rounding in base-10 notation is done by raising the last figure by 1 if the next figure would be equal to or greater than 5, e.g. $\frac{2}{3}$ becomes 0.666667 to 6 decimal places.

Rounding in binary notation is done by raising the last figure by 1 if the next figure would have been 1, e.g. $\frac{2}{3}$ becomes 0.101011 to 6 places.

Overflow Overflow occurs when the result of a calculation is too large for the storage space reserved for it. In a digital computer only a certain number of bits are used to store any given number. For example, if a register uses 8 bits, using the twos complement method of representation, then the range of numbers which can be stored is from − 128 to + 127.

sign digit ↓	64	32	16	8	4	2	1	
0	1	1	1	1	1	1	1	largest number (+ 127)
1	0	0	0	0	0	0	0	smallest number (− 128)

If the answer to a calculation is outside this range, an overflow occurs. An error message will usually be shown and the program is halted.

The bit size of registers governs the storage of large numbers. Registers are usually 8-bit, 16-bit or 32-bit, depending on the architecture of the computer.

Underflow *Underflow* occurs when the result of a calculation is too small for the range of the number representation being used.

3 Computer Logic

Computer Logic Most computer circuitry consists of electrical circuits with voltages at one of two levels:

- logic 0 = 0 volts (or slightly over);
- logic 1 = 5 volts (or slightly under).

Logic Gates Small electronic components are used to make up serial and parallel switching circuits. These are known as *logic gates*. A logic gate is a circuit with *one or more inputs* and with *only one output*.

There are four widely used logic gates:

- AND gate;
- OR gate;
- EXCLUSIVE-OR gate;
- NOT gate

AND Gate Two inputs both set at 1 are needed to produce an output of 1.

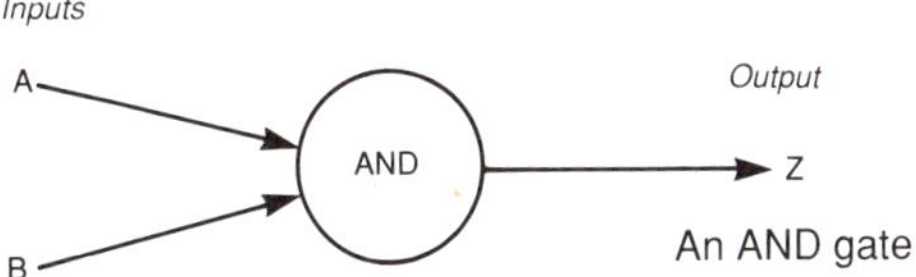

An AND gate

Truth Tables A *truth table* shows the outputs from a logic circuit for all the possible combinations of the inputs.

Truth table for an AND gate

input	input	output
A	B	Z
0	0	0
0	1	0
1	0	0
1	1	1

OR Gate Either one of two inputs must be set at 1 to give an output of 1.

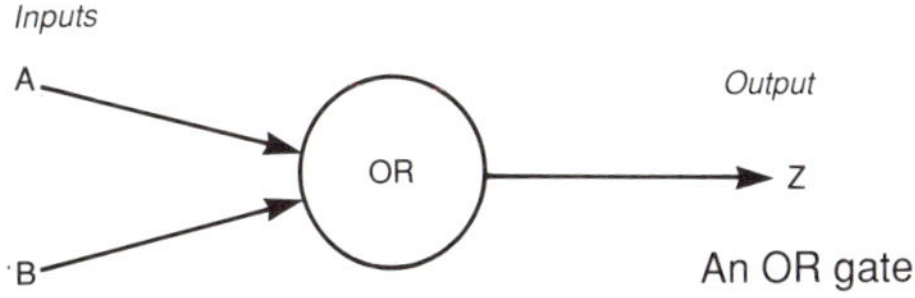

An OR gate

Truth Table for an OR Gate

input	input	output
A	B	Z
0	0	0
0	1	1
1	0	1
1	1	1

Exclusive-OR Gate The output is 1 when *either* of the two inputs is 1, but *not if both are 1.*

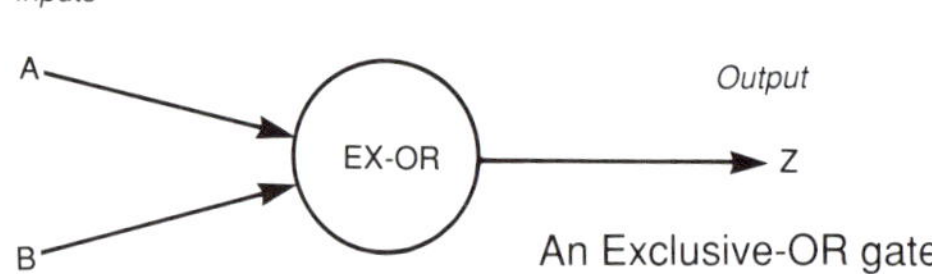

An Exclusive-OR gate

Truth Table for an Exclusive-OR Gate

input	input	output
A	B	Z
0	0	0
0	1	1
1	0	1
1	1	0

NOT Gate A NOT gate, or *inverter*, has only one input and it changes the signal to its opposite.

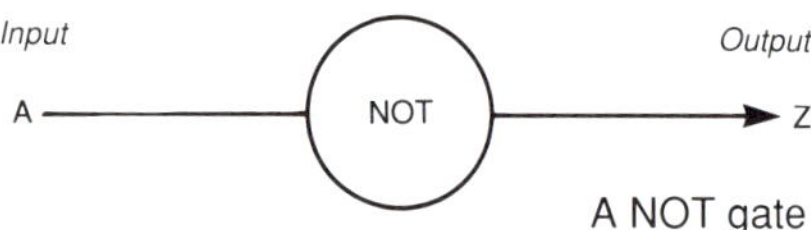

A NOT gate

Truth Table for a NOT Gate

input	output
A	Z
0	1
1	0

Logic Circuits Truth tables can be built up for larger, more complicated circuits.

Let us look at the following example.

In this example there are three inputs A, B and C and one output Z.

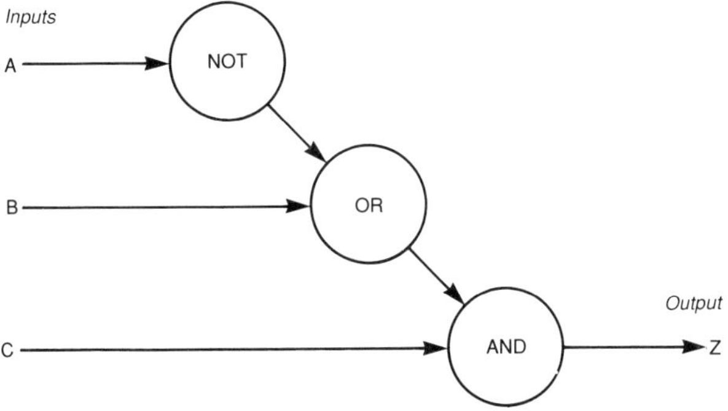

The first thing to do is to write down all the possible inputs in binary form, starting with 000. Here there will be eight possible combinations.

input A	input B	input C
0	0	0
0	0	1
0	1	0
0	1	1
1	0	0
1	0	1
1	1	0
1	1	1

Next we need to work out the outputs from each gate.

It is a good idea to write numbers over each gate to get the order correct and to give the intermediate outputs from each gate a separate letter.

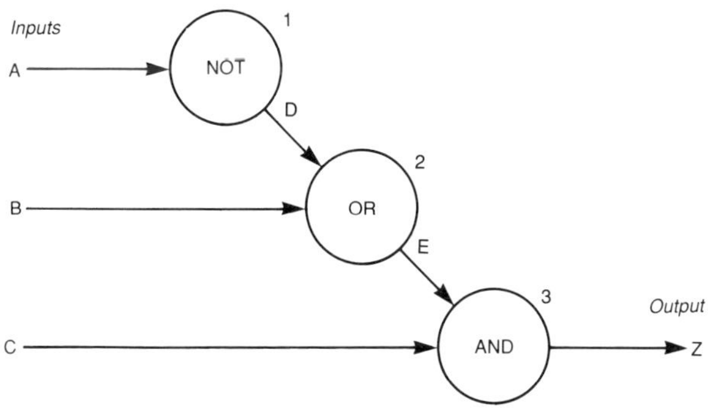

The intermediate outputs from each gate can be worked out and filled in on the truth table.

input	input	input	output	output
A	B	C	D	E
0	0	0	1	1
0	0	1	1	1
0	1	0	1	1
0	1	1	1	1
1	0	0	0	0
1	0	1	0	0
1	1	0	0	1
1	1	1	0	1

Using the intermediate outputs, the possible output for Z can then be worked out.

input	input	input	output	output	output
A	B	C	D	E	Z
0	0	0	1	1	0
0	0	1	1	1	1
0	1	0	1	1	0
0	1	1	1	1	1
1	0	0	0	0	0
1	0	1	0	0	0
1	1	0	0	1	0
1	1	1	0	1	1

Worked Logic Example

A chemical plant is controlled automatically by a logic network.

There are three binary signals which have the following values under certain conditions.

Signal	Binary Value	Condition
T	1	Temperature = or > than 180°C
	0	Temperature < 180°C
P	1	Pressure > 200 atmospheres
	0	Pressure = or < 200 atmospheres
C	1	Carbon Dioxide concentration > 70%
	0	Carbon Dioxide concentration < or = 70%

An alarm sounds (Z=1) whenever either of the following conditions arise:

(i) The temperature is equal to or greater than 180°C and the carbon dioxide concentration is equal to or less than 70%.

(ii) The pressure is greater than 200 atmospheres and the carbon dioxide concentration is greater than 70%.

Complete the following truth table for this system.

T	P	C	Z
0	0	0	
0	0	1	
0	1	0	
0	1	1	
1	0	0	
1	0	1	
1	1	0	
1	1	1	

Solution The alarm will sound when:

(i) the temperature is equal to or greater than 180°C, i.e. T=1,

AND

the carbon dioxide concentration is less than or equal to 70%, i.e. C=0

OR

(ii) the pressure is greater than 200 atmospheres, i.e. P=1,

AND

the carbon dioxide concentration is greater than 70%, i.e. C=1.

So

Z=1 when T=1 AND C=0

OR

Z=1 when P=1 AND C=1.

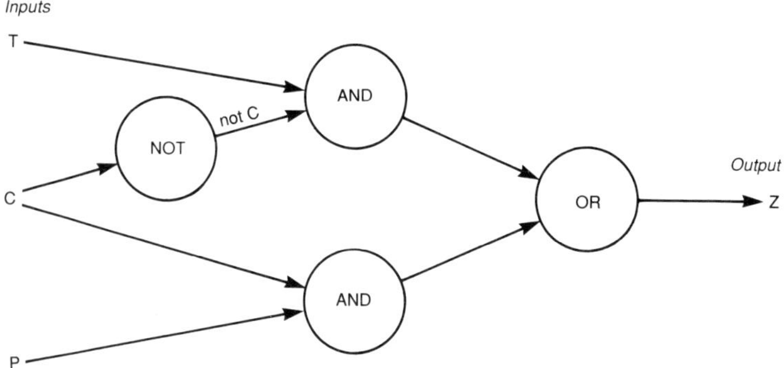

Go through the truth table and fill in Z = 1 for the above conditions. All the rest will be 0.

T	P	C	Z
0	0	0	0
0	0	1	0
0	1	0	0
0	1	1	1
1	0	0	1
1	0	1	0
1	1	0	1
1	1	1	1

4 Input Devices

Input Devices An *input device* is a piece of machinery or *hardware* which transmits input data to the computer. It changes the input data into a form that the computer can understand.

Punched Card (outdated) Punched cards normally have 80 columns and 12 rows, allowing the storage of 80 characters, each having 12 bits.

Cards often have the actual characters written at the top of the card above each column.

Advantages:

- Punched cards are cheap to use.

Disadvantages:

- Punched cards have limited capacity as they can hold only 80 characters per card.
- They are bulky.
- Input speeds are slow.
- It is easy to lose cards, or mix them up.
- The card reader creates a lot of dust.

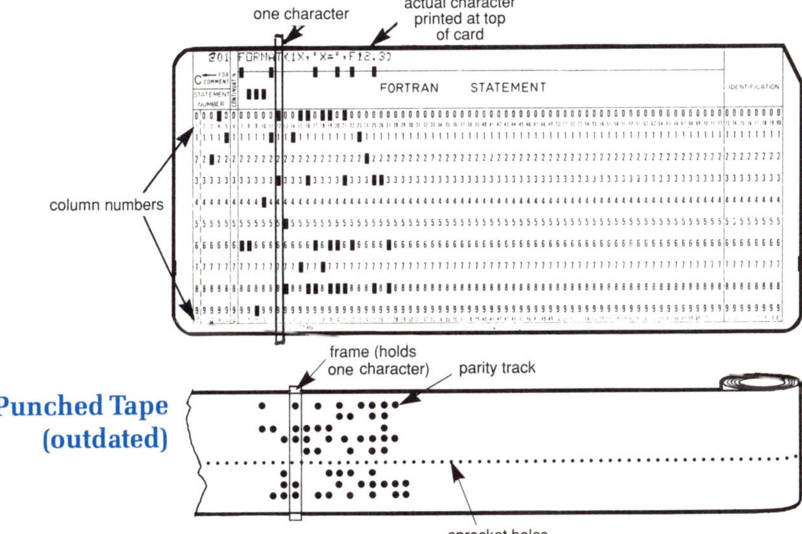

Punched Tape (outdated)

Punched tape has 6, 7 or 8 tracks, with an area for each character called a *frame*. One track is often a *parity* track with holes punched in it to produce 'odd' or 'even' parity. This is a checking method to ensure that data is transmitted correctly.

Advantages:

- Punched tape has unlimited capacity.
- It is not as bulky as punched cards.
- It allows variable-length records.
- It is easy to store.

Disadvantages:

- Punched tape has a very slow input speed.
- It cannot be sorted off-line.
- Insertions and deletions generally entail the preparation of a new tape.

Card Punch or Paper Tape Punch

A *card punch* or *paper tape punch* consists of a keyboard where each key operates a series of punch knives which strike the card or tape, producing holes in the appropriate positions.

Verifier

A *verifier* is a device which carries out checks for data preparation errors. It consists of a keyboard which the operator uses to type out data which is simultaneously compared with previously prepared input media (i.e. card or tape). If a mismatch occurs, the process is stopped and the error corrected.

It reduces preparation error substantially but is costly and time consuming as the data is effectively keyed in twice.

Card or Tape Reader

A *card* or *tape reader* converts patterns of holes to patterns of electrical pulses. Cards or tape are fed automatically from a hopper or a reel and pass over a light on one side and photoelectric cells on the other.

Card readers read at approximately 400 cards per minute (with up to 80 characters per card, i.e. around 500 characters per second).

Tape readers read at approximately 60 to 6000 characters per second.

Document Readers

A *document reader* records information straight from a *source document*. No *data preparation* is involved.

Types of Document Reader

There are four types of document reader:

- *Mark sense reader*;
- *Optical mark reader* (OMR);
- *Optical character reader* (OCR);
- *Magnetic ink character reader* (MICR).

Mark sensing and optical mark reading use the principle that positions on a document can be given certain values, and these positions, when marked, can be interpreted by a machine.

Mark Sense Readers

Mark sense readers can accept forms on which data has been entered by means of a set of pencil marks. The marks are detected electronically, as the graphite in the pencil mark will conduct electricity between two contacts, thus completing the circuit.

Optical Mark Readers (OMR)

Optical mark readers can detect a break in the reflected light.

The above two types of reader are used in situations where the data to be input is simple and the volume of data is large enough to justify the cost of designing the documents.

Examples of use include:

meter reader documents (these are known as *turnaround documents*, which are produced as output at one stage of the data-processing cycle and, after data is added to them, they are used as input for further processing);

football pools coupons;

multiple-choice examination answer sheets.

Advantages:

- The documents can be prepared where the data originates.

Disadvantages:

- The verification of marked data is difficult.
- Training may be necessary to explain how to fill in the documents correctly.
- A change in document design will require the reprogramming of the document reader.
- The cost of the readers is relatively high.

Optical Character Recognition (OCR) Alphabetic and numeric characters are created in a particular type style which can be read by a special machine and which also can be understood by humans. The system is suitable for turnaround documents and is used for:

gas and electricity billing;
insurance premium renewals;
Giro forms.

0 1 2 3 4 5 6 7 8 9
A B C D E F G H I J
K L M N O P Q R S T
U V W X Y Z

0 1 2 3 4 5 6 7 8 9
A B C D E F G H I J
K L M N O P Q R S T
U V W X Y Z

Two common OCR character sets

Advantages:

- As no transcript is required, there is no chance of error in data preparation.

Disadvantages:

- A high standard of optical characters and documents is required to avoid error rejections.
- The cost of the readers is relatively high.

Magnetic Ink Character Recognition (MICR) Characters are printed in a special ink which can be magnetised. This system is used mainly on cheques and the characters are decipherable both by computers and by humans. No transcription is required and so there are few errors in data preparation.

The data coded includes the serial number of the cheque, the bank account number and the bank sort code. The amount written on to the cheque is encoded on to it by the first bank to receive the cheque. The cheque can then be input to the computer.

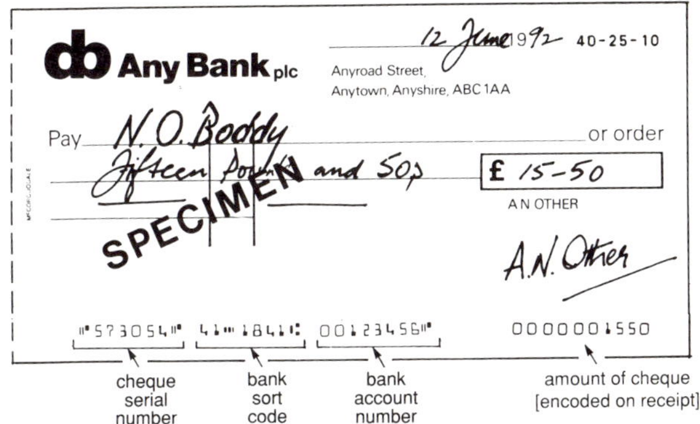

Advantages:

- The information is readable by machine and by humans.
- It allows fast processing.
- Cheques can be folded, handled and stamped without affecting the encoded data.
- It makes forgery difficult.

Disadvantages:

- Only a small character set is used, all numeric.

Bar Codes/ Magnetic Strips

Data can be recorded on small strips which are read optically or magnetically.

Optical reading is done by using printed bar codes, i.e. alternating lines and spaces which represent data in binary. Magnetic reading is done from a strip of magnetic tape on which data has been encoded.

9 780721 746210

The bar code from this book

In each case data is read by a *wand* or *light pen*, or the code is passed over a laser bar code reader which is usually set in a counter.

Both bar codes and magnetic strips are used for stock recording and at shop checkouts.

Advantages:

- No transcription is required.
- It saves the checkout worker a lot of time and effort.

Disadvantages:

- The initial outlay for the reading equipment is expensive.

Kimball Tags A *Kimball tag* is a ticket which is used frequently in fashion shops. The tag is attached to a garment by the manufacturer and contains a variety of data, e.g. size, description, price code. This information is printed on the tags for the benefit of the sales assistant and customer, but is coded in the form of holes punched into the label or on magnetic strips or bar codes for use by the computer.

When an item is sold, the sales assistant removes the tag. At the end of the day, these tags are sent off to the firm's computer centre where they are read by a document reader. Alternatively, the magnetic strip tags may be read using a special wand attached to a point-of-sale (POS) terminal. The information obtained from the tags is used for stock re-ordering and for sales reports.

Advantages:

- Data is captured at source.
- Data collection is done mainly by machine, therefore there is less chance of error.
- The sales assistant's job is simplified as data is already recorded.

Disadvantages:

- There are limits to the amount of data which can be stored on the tags.
- Problems may arise if the price of goods is reduced, but if the price is in a code this can be overcome.
- Tags are small and present handling problems.

Voice Input As human speech varies in accent, pitch and personal style, this makes voice recognition by computer very difficult. Computers are not able, at present, to understand continuous spoken language. They can recognise a limited number of words spoken by a known speaker.

Direct Data Entry (DDE) Direct data entry allows the data items to be keyed in and then verified before being collated for further processing.

Methods of Direct Data Entry

There are three methods of direct data entry:

- *key-to-disk*;
- *key-to-tape*;
- *key-to-cassette*.

Key-to-Disk

Several key stations are linked to a processor and have simultaneous access to disk for entry of data. Data is transferred by the processor, after verification, to one tape reel under the control of a supervisor (see page 65).

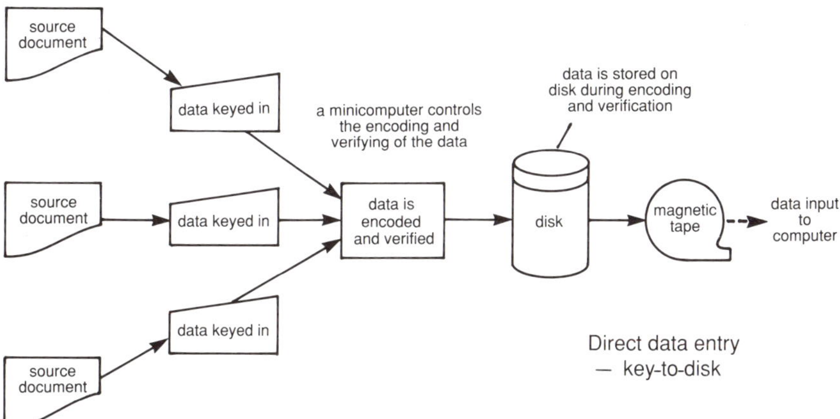

Direct data entry — key-to-disk

Advantages:

- A certain amount of validation (see page 80) can be done off-line.
- It is possible to incorporate control totals, i.e. subtotals of the number of data transactions in each batch.
- Error correction is easily accomplished.
- Once data has been keyed on to the disk, verification can be carried out from any of the key stations.

Disadvantages:

- All key stations are linked to one processor. If the processor breaks down, all processing stops.
- A high capital outlay is required, so large volumes of data have to be processed to justify this system.
- Data tends not to be so carefully prepared.

Key-to-Tape This uses separate machines (called *encoders*) which consist of a keyboard, a small memory and a reel of magnetic tape. Data is keyed on to tape via the encoder's memory. Some validation can be done whilst the data is in memory.

When a batch of documents has been encoded on to tape, verification follows. Reels from a number of encoders are merged on to one reel. The spooled reel is then used as input to the computer.

Advantages:

- Data is encoded directly on to magnetic tape.
- Error correction is simple to do.

Disadvantages:

- Tapes have to be spooled before input, which is time consuming.
- Tapes have to be reloaded to be verified, which is also time consuming.
- This system is not as flexible as key-to-disk in terms of program capability.
- Verification has to be done by a shift supervisor re-keying the data.

Key-to-Cassette This system is used in shops for daily transactions. A short reel of tape in a plastic housing is fitted into a point-of-sale terminal. As goods are sold, the data is keyed in and is recorded on to the cassette. At the end of the day the cassette is sent off to the main data-processing office and, before being input to the mainframe, several cassettes are combined on to a large reel of magnetic tape.

Advantages:

- The system is cheap.

Disadvantages:

- Staff training is necessary to ensure that data is keyed in correctly.

Joystick A *joystick* is a small lever which can be moved in various directions and is used to control computer games.

Mouse A *mouse* is a small hand-held device. It has a moving ball underneath, a button switch and a 'tail' which is

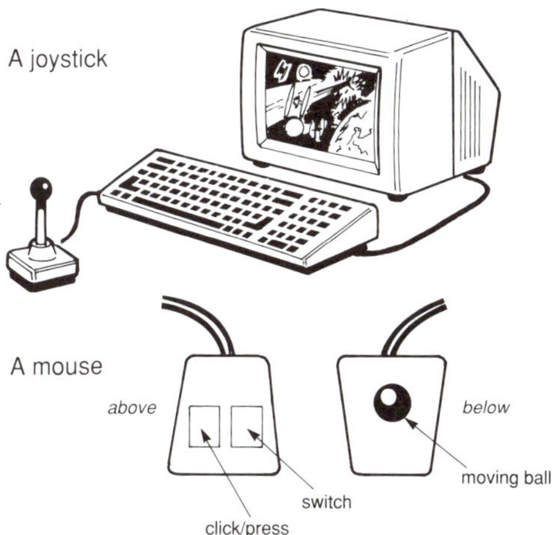

a cable connected to the computer. The ball underneath the mouse is moved around on the surface of the desk and, as it moves, a corresponding pointer or *cursor* moves on the computer screen. The pointer and the button switch are used to select options from a menu or program.

Digitiser A *digitiser* is a round object which is moved by hand on a special type of pad. As it moves, a pointer moves on the screen in the corresponding position. A digitiser is more precise than a mouse. It is, however, more expensive. Digitisers are used in the input of drawings, designs and architects' plans.

5 Output Devices

Output Devices An *output device* is a piece of hardware which changes machine language into a form recognisable by humans. Output can be of two types:

- For use at a later date by the computer. It can be output on to magnetic tape or disk for input later as required.
- For direct use by the user, e.g. printouts, or the data could be used to control devices, e.g. a plotter or machine tools.

Line Printer *Line printers* are used with mini and mainframe computers. They print a complete line at a time and are used for large volumes of printing.

Advantages:

- Line printers are very quick.
- They produce good quality printout.

Disadvantages:

- Line printers are large, noisy and expensive.

There are two main types of line printer:
barrel printers and *chain printers*.

The speeds of both these types of printer vary from 400 to 3000 lines per minute.

Barrel Printer A *barrel printer* consists of a rapidly rotating cylinder with a complete row of each character across its surface.

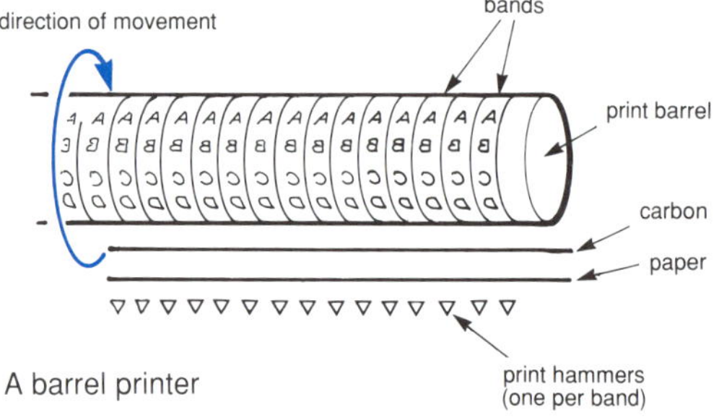

A barrel printer

Printing a line takes one complete revolution of the barrel. Thus any As on the line are printed first, then the Bs, etc., e.g. DATA would be printed in the following order

```
   A     A
D  A     A
D  A  T  A
```

Chain Printer A *chain printer* consists of a rapidly moving chain carrying several sets of characters. As a character passes the position where it is to be printed, a hammer hits the paper and carbon against the character.

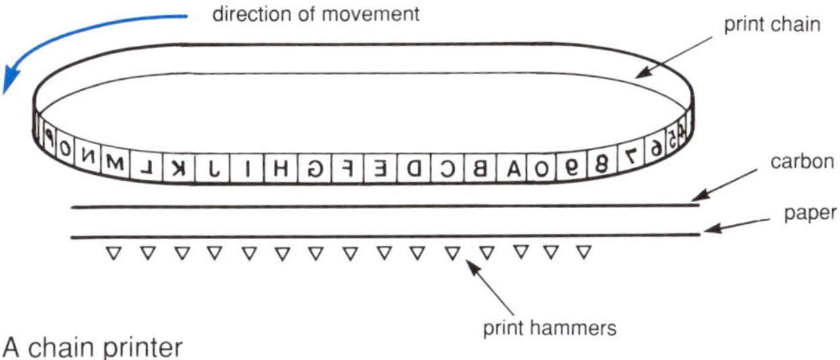

A chain printer

Dot-matrix Printer *Dot-matrix printers* are faster than typewriters, but not as fast as line printers. Speeds of about 100 characters per second at 120 characters per line give the dot-matrix printer a speed of about 50 lines per minute. Each character is formed by a series of dots, produced by fine needles, arranged in a matrix usually with 5 columns and 7 rows. Different combinations of needles produce different characters.

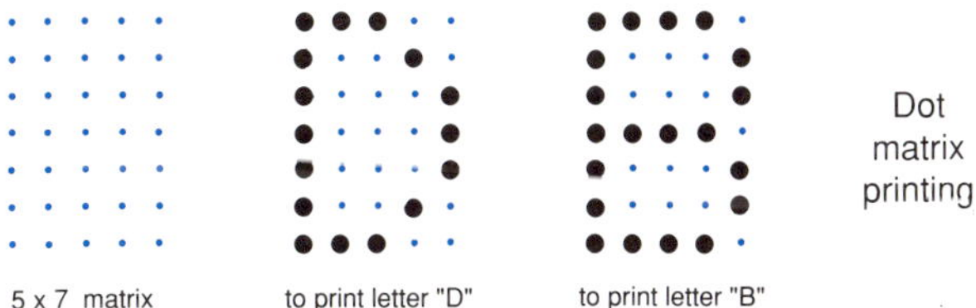

Dot matrix printing

Advantages:

- Dot-matrix printers are relatively quick and relatively cheap.

Disadvantages:

- They are noisy and the printing quality is not high.

Daisy-wheel Printer With a *daisy-wheel printer* characters are arranged near the ends of the spokes of a rimless wheel, like the petals of a daisy. These wheels are interchangeable, allowing alternative character sets. They are solid fonts, i.e. each character is continuous and not made up of tiny dots. Daisy-wheel printers are used for office computer systems.

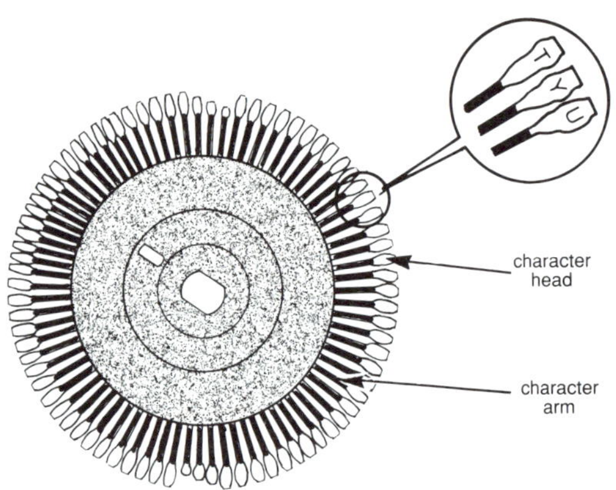

Advantages:

- Daisy-wheel printers give a high-quality printout.
- They are quieter than a dot-matrix printer.

Disadvantages:

- They are slow.
- They are more expensive than a dot-matrix printer.

Golf-ball Printer A *golf-ball printer* is similar to the daisy-wheel printer, but the print head is a moveable sphere with the characters arranged around it.

Thermal Printer With a *thermal printer*, a heated print head is used to print dot-matrix characters on to specially treated paper.

Advantages:

- They are quick.

Disadvantages:

- They require expensive special paper which is sometimes of a poor texture.

Ink-jet Printer With an *ink-jet printer*, hollow needles are used to squirt ink on to the paper in a dot-matrix style.

Advantages:

- They are quiet.

Disadvantages:

- They require ink all the time, therefore the holes must be kept clean.

Laser Page Printer *A laser printer* forms a page of print by projecting a beam of light on to an electrostatic drum. This collects ink in the shape of the projected characters and prints them. Laser printers are limited by the mechanical speeds of paper movement. They can print 150 pages per minute (between 10 500 and 30 000 lines per minute – equivalent to printing a small novel in 2 minutes!).

Advantages:

- They are very fast.
- They produce good print quality.

Disadvantages:

- They are very expensive.
- They require special paper.
- They are noisy due to the speed of paper movement.

Office Laser Printers There are laser printers small enough to use in an office which are more expensive than dot-matrix and daisy-wheel printers, but which are very fast and produce good quality printing including graphics.

Advantages:

- They are quiet.
- They can produce good quality printing.
- They can produce graphics also.

Disadvantages:

- They are expensive.

Graph Plotters *Graph plotters* are also known as *digital plotters* or *XY plotters*. They are used to produce drawings, charts, maps, graphs, for design engineering and for architectural drawings.

Advantages:

- Complex diagrams can be produced.
- Several different colours can be used.

Disadvantages:

- They are very slow and are expensive.

There are two main types of graph plotter: *drum plotters* and *flat-bed plotters*.

Drum Plotter

A *drum plotter* consists of a roll of special paper which moves forwards and backwards through the plotter while a pen moves across the paper. This combination of paper and pen movement allows lines in any direction or any letter to be drawn.

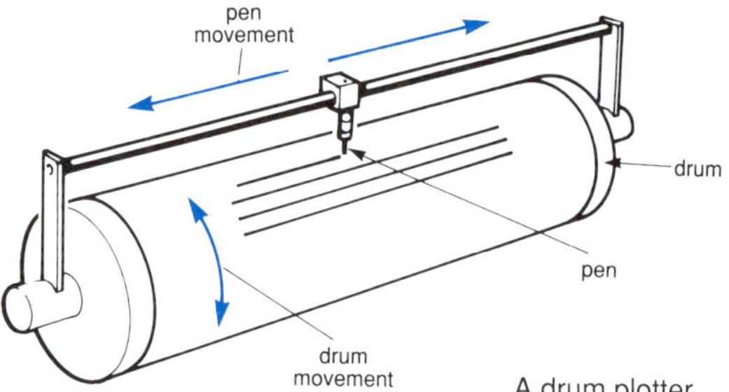

A drum plotter

Advantages:

- Complex diagrams can be produced.
- Several different colours can be used.

Disadvantages:

- They are very slow and are expensive.

Flat Bed Plotter

In a *flat bed plotter* the paper is held flat and still while the pen moves in all directions.

Pen colour changes can be made when the pen is raised up from the paper.

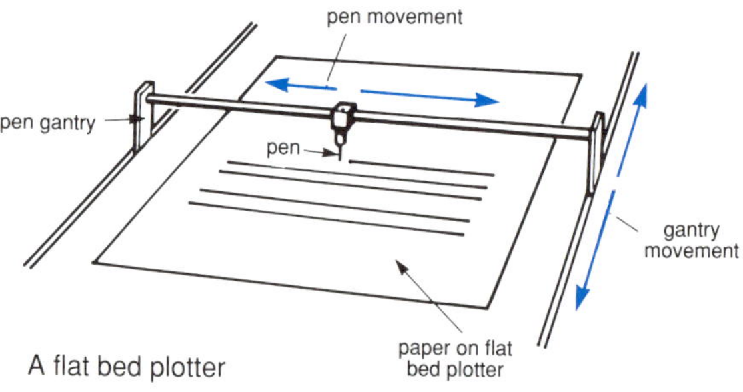

A flat bed plotter

Visual Display Unit (VDU) A *visual display unit* consists of a monitor screen like a television (but with a better resolution, i.e. a sharper picture). Output characters are displayed on a screen. A VDU is used in an interactive situation where high speed of output is necessary but hard copy is not required, and where the noise of printing would be a nuisance.

Advantages:

- VDUs provide virtually instant output.
- They are quiet in use.

Disadvantages:

- No hard copy is produced, so any output is temporary.

Computer Output on Microfilm/ Microfiche (COM) Here, output is recorded in a much reduced form on high-quality film. The output can be placed on to either microfilm or microfiche.

COM is used in libraries for catalogues and in garages for listing the car parts which are available.

Microfilm *Microfilm* is a continuous reel of film.

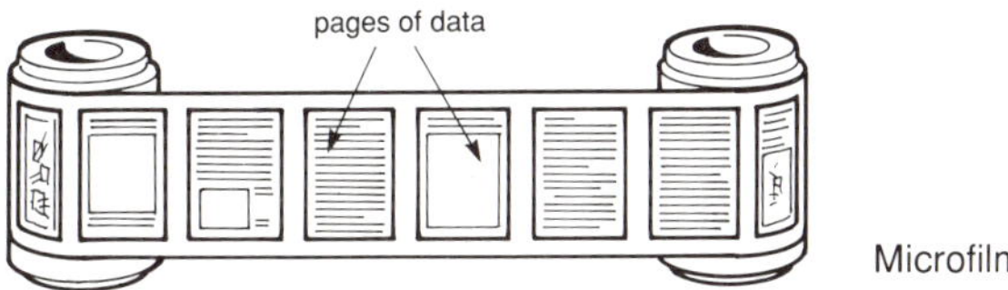

Microfilm

Microfiche *Microfiche* is a rectangular sheet of film large enough to contain a number of pages of data.

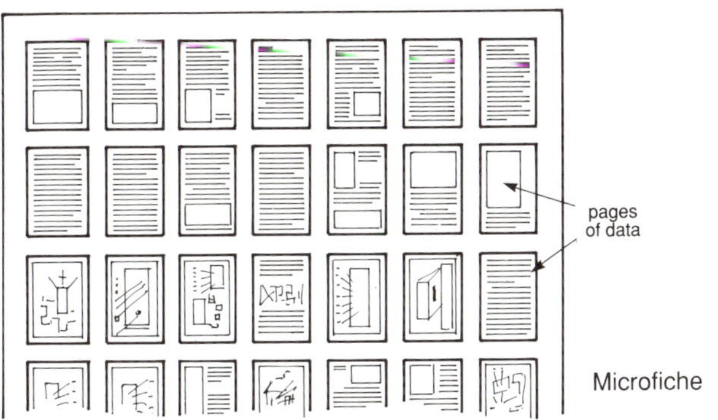

Microfiche

Advantages:
COM is:
- fast and cheap to produce;
- compact, taking up less storage space than full-sized documents;
- easily distributed by post;
- good for archive storage.

Disadvantages:
- COM requires a special reader.
- It cannot be amended by hand.

Voice Output This type of output is developing with pre-recorded phrases or 'synthesised' voices created by storing word patterns.

Advantages:
- No reading ability is required.
- It can easily be accessed by telephone.

Disadvantages:
- Voice output is not suitable for use in a noisy environment.
- The output is not permanent.
- Any words not understood have to be repeated by the computer.

6 Backing Storage

Backing Storage *Backing storage* is used to retain a large amount of information, either programs or data, on a permanent basis.

There are two categories of backing storage: *random (or direct) access* and *serial (or sequential) access*.

Random Access Random or direct access is the process of retrieving data items without the necessity of reading any other stored data first.

Serial Access Serial access is the process of retrieving items of data by first reading through all the previous items. (Sequential access is the same, except that the data is organised in a predetermined manner.)

Reasons for Using Backing Storage CPU memory is:

- expensive;
- limited in capacity;
- often *volatile*, i.e. the content is lost when the power is switched off.

Magnetic Backing Storage Magnetic tapes and disks are the main types of backing storage although paper tape and punched cards are still used occasionally.

Magnetic Tapes Magnetic tapes allow serial or sequential access only.

The tape is usually between 0.38 cm and 2.54 cm wide, the most common type being 1.27 cm wide. Tapes are up to 730 metres in length. They are made of plastic and are coated on one side with iron oxide which can be magnetised in one of two directions to store a 0 or a 1.

Information is stored across the width of the tape.

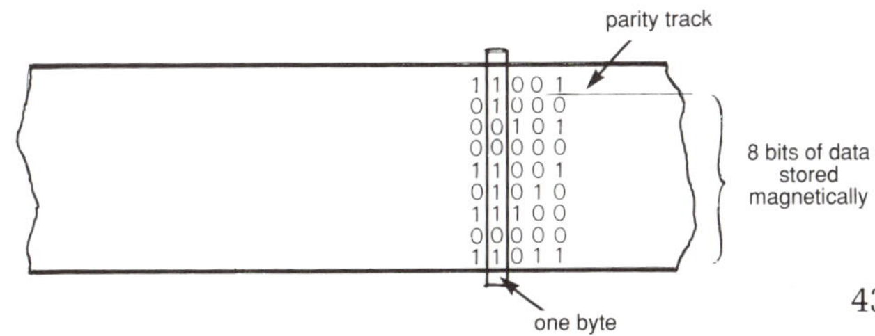

Parity Tapes have a *parity track* which is a checking system used to ensure that the data is not corrupted.

Packing Density The packing density of a magnetic tape is 720 characters per centimetre. One tape can store up to 50 000 000 characters.

Temperature Temperature must be kept constant, as an expansion or contraction of the tape may cause the tightly packed magnetic areas to be distorted, corrupting the data.

Blocks Data is stored in *blocks*, separated by *interblock gaps*. Data is read whilst the tape is moving at full speed, and data is transferred from the tape to main memory one block at a time. The tape is stopped whilst the CPU processes the data. The interblock gap allows the tape to decelerate and accelerate again to the correct speed for data transfer.

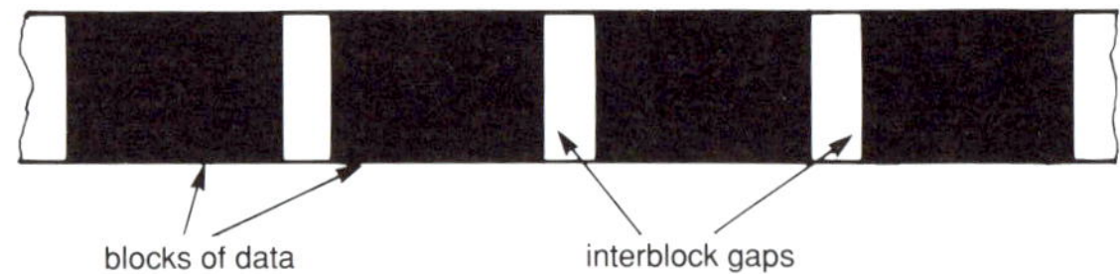

Advantages of Tapes

- Tapes are cheaper than disks.
- Tape units are cheaper than disk drives.
- Tapes take up less space and are easier to store than disks.
- They are best used when vast quantities of data have to be stored.

Disadvantages of Tapes

- Tapes allow serial access only.
- Tapes wear out after a time.
- Tapes are vulnerable to dust and changes in temperature and humidity.
- Tapes need to be used in an expensive air-conditioned environment and have to be protected from stray magnetic fields.
- Tapes need to be handled carefully to avoid grease and creasing, but many tapes are now self-loading.

Magnetic Tape Unit A *magnetic tape unit* is a device which transfers data to or from a magnetic tape. It consists of two spools, one for the supply reel and one for the take-up reel, and wheels which pass the tape over a read/write and erase head. So as not to damage the tape whilst stopping and starting at high speeds, and to keep the tape at the proper tension, vacuum columns are used to allow some slack in the tape beneath each reel. Data is transferred at around 100 000 characters per second.

The tape can go in only one direction, so data can be processed only in serial mode.

Tapes are used for batch processing (see page 76).

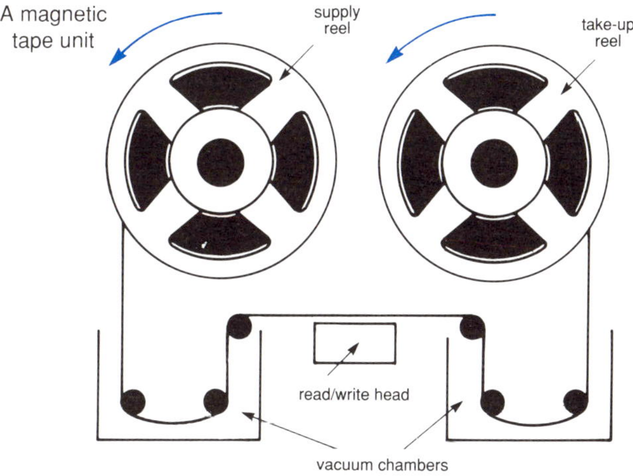

Write Permit Ring A *write permit ring* (see also page 86), which is a circle of plastic inserted into the back of a reel of tape, prevents the overwriting of data on a tape. Without this, data cannot be written to a tape.

Magnetic Disks Magnetic disks allow random access. They are made of metal and are coated with a substance which can be magnetised. They are used either singly, or in packs of 6 or 10 mounted on one shaft. The top and bottom surfaces of the disk packs are not used, as they are more likely to be damaged by dust or touch. Some disk packs are fixed in place in the disk drive, while others may be removed (*exchangeable disk packs*).

Tracks and Sectors Small areas can be magnetised in one of two directions to store a 0 or a 1. These areas are arranged around the disk in concentric *tracks*. These tracks are divided into *sectors* with gaps between them.

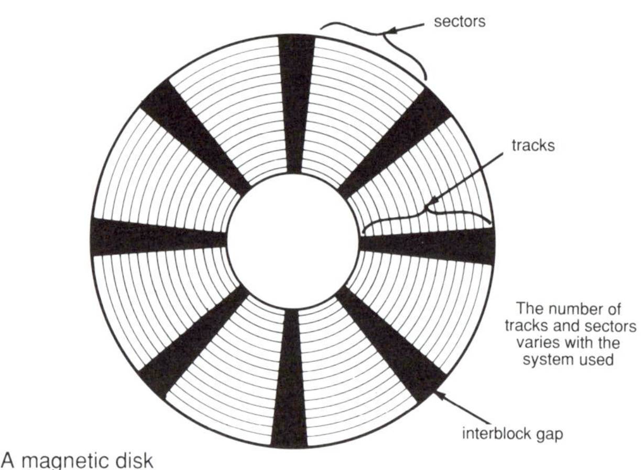

A magnetic disk

Formatting New disks need to be *formatted* before use. This means that the computer's operating system allocates the position of the tracks and sectors as used by the system.

Each track contains the same number of stored characters, so tracks nearer the centre are more closely packed than the outer ones.

Cylinders Tracks above one another are called a *cylinder*.

Capacity A disk can store up to 300 megabytes.

Disk Drive A *disk drive* is a device which transfers data to and from a magnetic disk. The disk or disk pack is rotated at approximately 3000 revolutions per minute. The read/write heads are floating on a cushion of air very close to the surface of the disk.

Disks should not be exposed to dust, so the drives are enclosed. Disk drives read data at 150 000 characters per second. Data can only be read when the disk is at full speed.

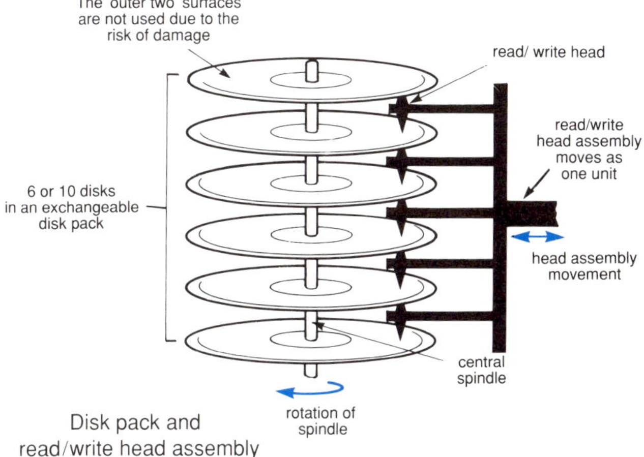

Disk pack and read/write head assembly

The heads move in together and data is written to and read from all the tracks in one cylinder at the same time.

Data is addressable, i.e. it may be accessed by its track number, sector number and, if necessary, cylinder number.

Advantages of Disks

- They allow random access to data. (Both random access and serial access are possible, depending on how the data has been stored.
- Random access allows for transaction processing (see page 78), so that updating in place is possible.

Disadvantages of Disks

- Disks are more expensive than tapes.
- Disk drives are more expensive than tape units.
- Disks are more difficult to store than tapes.

Floppy Disks

Floppy disks are made of thin, flexible plastic, usually coated on both sides with a magnetisable material, although sometimes only one side is used. They are used in personal computers and can store between 360 kilobytes and 2 megabytes. They rotate at approximately 300 revolutions per minute. They are easily damaged by poor handling and should always be kept in their protective card or plastic envelopes when not in use. Some are kept permanently in hard plastic cases.

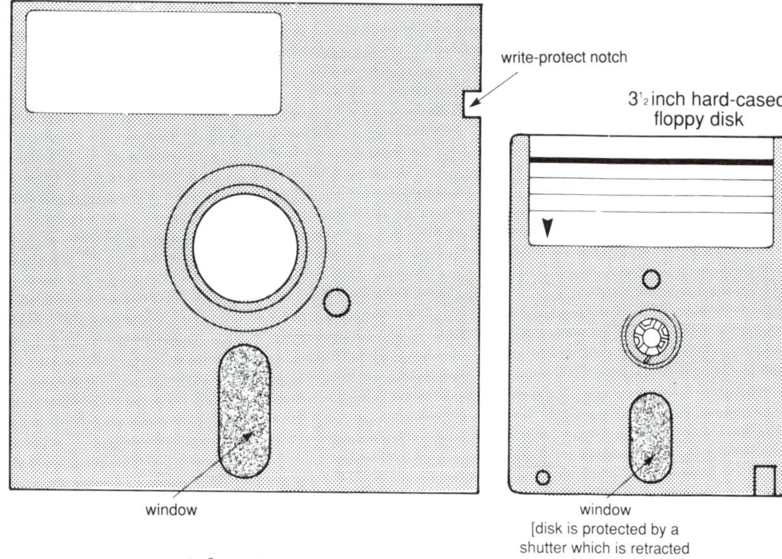

Advantages:

- They are cheap and can be transported easily, e.g. by post.

Disadvantages:

- They can be destroyed, lost or stolen easily.
- The read/write heads touch the disks which causes them to wear out.
- They have a relatively small capacity.

Magnetic Cards *Magnetic cards* are like punched cards, except that they use magnetised areas instead of holes. They allow random access.

Cassettes Cassettes are ordinary audio cassettes. Data is read from and written to them using cassette recorders. They are used mainly with microcomputers in use in homes and at point-of-sale terminals. The speed of transfer is very slow at just a few characters per second.

Magnetic Bubble Memory A *magnetic bubble memory* consists of a bubble or blob of magnetism in a crystal of garnet which can be given different directions to indicate 0 or 1. It is slower than a semi-conductor memory but is non-volatile.

Optical Disks On *optical disks*, programs and data are stored in a binary coding as small indentations on the surface of the disk. The recording of the data and the reading of the disk are done by means of a laser beam. At present, this is read-only memory as the data cannot be erased or rewritten. Optical disks are used to store archives of data and for training material for use with interactive video.

Advantages:

Optical disks:

- have a high storage capacity, e.g. 50 gigabytes;
- provide a high quality of pictures and sound;
- allow fast random access, though not as fast as from magnetic hard disk;
- have a long life as there is no mechanical/physical contact between the disk and the optical reading system;
- are difficult to copy, which is an advantage where copyright is concerned.

Disadvantages:

- The hardware for reading optical disks is expensive.
- It is expensive to produce a master disk.
- There is very little software available at present.
- They are read-only at present.

Interactive Video *Interactive video* uses the advantages of optical disks and computers to give rapid random access (unlike video tapes) and interactive viewing. A video disk can store text, images and audio signals and is of use in advertising, training and education.

Which Method of Backing Storage to Use The size and nature of the computer system and the type of data processing being done dictates which method is used. The main considerations are:

- cost;
- method of access;
- speed of transfer.

7 Modes of Computer Operation

Modes of Computer Operation The following modes of computer operation are not necessarily mutually exclusive.

On-line Being *on-line* describes when a device is directly connected to a computer and is under its control, e.g. a printer in use is said to be on-line.

Off-line When a task is performed *off-line* it means that the devices used are not connected to the computer, e.g. the preparation of some input documents is done off-line.

Interactive Processing *Interactive processing* occurs when a 'conversation' situation is set up between the computer and the user, e.g. when using a microcomputer via a keyboard and a VDU.

Batch Processing During *batch processing*, transactions are kept together and then input for processing to the computer all in one batch. This type of processing is used for a monthly payroll run, or quarterly gas and electricity billing.

Transaction Processing With *transaction processing*, transactions are processed as and when they occur, e.g. hotel reservations, airline bookings.

Multi-access *Multi-access* occurs when the programs which are running in a multi-programming situation are interactive. In a multi-access system, a number of users with terminals *appear* to use the computer at the same time.

A common way of providing multi-access is by time-sharing. Each user is allocated a short time slice which is long enough for the user to appear to have continuous use of the system. A typical time slice is 1/50th of a second.

An airline flight-booking system could use a multi-access system.

Remote Access *Remote access* is access to a computer which is in a geographically different place. This link can be achieved using modems and a telephone line.

Real Time *Real time* is a term now used to describe output from an analogue computer, e.g. a signal on an oscilloscope screen. It means that values are output as and when they are calculated, without any delay, e.g. process control in manufacture, engine management chips in cars. The computer is dealing with what is actually happening.

Multi-Programming (Multi-tasking) In a *multi-programming* system the computer works on several programs at a time. Two or more programs are running apparently simultaneously and are sharing the use of peripherals. In fact, the processor can execute only one program at a time, working on one and then another in short bursts. Whilst one program is waiting for an input or output operation to be performed, another may have access to the CPU.

Networking In a *networking* system many terminals are linked together to one CPU, or several computers are linked to one main controlling computer.

Network structures

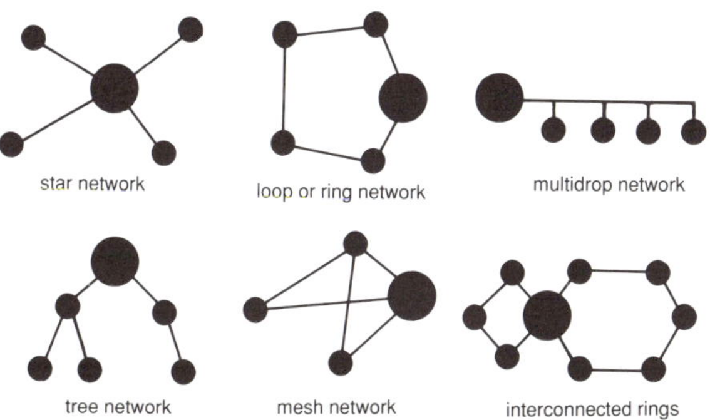

Types of Network There are two types of computer networks:

Local Area Networks (LAN) and *Wide Area Networks (WAN)*.

Local Area Networks (*LAN*) These are used to connect computers in a single room or to connect computers in different rooms of a building or buildings on one site.

Wide Area Networks (WAN) These are used to connect computers on different sites or even in different parts of the world.

8 Data Communicatons

Data Communications (Data Comms)

When a user is some distance from the computer, in a different room, city or even country, a *data communications* system may be used for transmitting data to and from the computer.

The system links up hardware, software and telecommunications facilities. It may consist of a terminal in one office connected to a computer in a different part of the building, or it may be a very complex, nationwide system of interconnected computers and terminals.

Components of a Data Communications System

A data communications system consists of:

- a sender of data, e.g. person at a terminal;
- a communication link, e.g. telephone;
- a receiver of data, e.g. computer or person at a terminal.

A data communications system is made up of five basic types of hardware components:

- computers;
- communications processor (front-end processor);
- modems;
- data communication terminals;
- communication links.

Computers in Data Communications

There may be one or more computers in a data communications system. The main (host) computer will be concerned with the basic data-processing tasks whilst other smaller computers handle tasks such as message switching, communication processing or local processing (i.e. very small data-processing tasks).

Message Switching

Message switching is a method of gathering into batches, organising and storing conveniently sized sections of data so that they can be transmitted economically.

Communications Processor (Front End Processor)

The tasks of the communications processor include:

- connecting the main computer to communications links;
- *polling* (checking the status of) remote terminals to see if they are ready to send or receive messages;
- accepting incoming data, converting it if necessary into a format for the main computer and back again as output for the main computer;
- performing store-and-forward functions by storing messages sent from one terminal to another when the second is busy, and forwarding them when the terminal is free;
- providing error detection and correction of incoming messages;
- logging messages in and out, both for audit and for restart purposes after a system 'crash';
- maintaining statistics concerning usage of the network.

Modems

Modems (*mo*dulator/*dem*odulators) change, or modulate, digital signals into analogue signals so that they can be sent by telephone, and then change them back into digital signals (demodulate) on receipt.

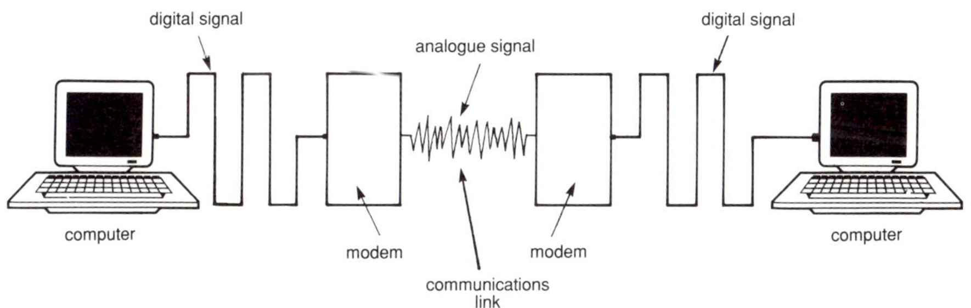

Data transmission via modems

Data Communications Terminals

Data communications terminals can be of various types:

- teletypewriters (becoming out of date);
- visual display units (VDUs);
- transacton terminals, e.g. bar code readers and keyboards at the point-of-sale;
- portable transaction terminals, often used for stock control.

Communication Links

Data is transmitted between remote terminals and computers by means of a communication link (channel) or network. Most organisations use the telephone network. There are five means of sending data, and the choice will depend on the distance involved:

- pairs of *copper wires* for local services;
- *microwaves* from tower to tower about 50 km apart;
- *copper coaxial cables* for long distance routes over land and sea;
- *optical fibres* for trunk and local services. The thin glass strands which make up these fibres are cheaper than copper and are not affected by electrical interference (this is important in factories);
- by *satellite* for very long distances.

Use of Data Communications

The most important uses of data communications by organisations are:

- enquiry/response;
- on-line data entry;
- remote job entry;
- conversational time-sharing;
- distributed processing.

Enquiry/Response

A request for information is usually made via a terminal with a VDU and the response should be received within seconds. Enquiry/response would include credit checking, law enforcement and library referencing.

On-line Data Entry

On-line data entry is used for transaction processing. Remote terminals, usually with VDUs, are placed in user departments and data is entered from these directly into the computer. Transactions may be entered as they occur. This type of entry is necessary when a computer database (see page 90) has to be kept up to date and where rapid response is required. It is used for reservation systems, for stock control, and by banks and building societies.

Remote Job Entry

A remote terminal and often a line printer are linked to a central computer. Batch jobs are entered and then transmitted to the main computer for processing. Results can be transmitted back to the remote site for display on the screen or for printing.

Conversational Time-sharing

Conversational time-sharing occurs when several users at remote locations can access a central computer. Responses are immediate and the user can interact with the computer in question-and-answer sessions.

Distributed Processing

Rather than using a large central computer, an organisation may use several smaller computers which are linked together by data communications. They may all share a single database. Data can be sent to and from head office or other branches as required. This is known as *distributed processing*.

Advantages of Data Communications

- The main processor itself does not have to be sited where the work is being done, and it can be accessed from several different places some distance away. Data can be captured at source in a computer-readable form, e.g. in a shop with a point-of-sales terminal.
- The speed of data transmission is far greater than if it had been sent by mail.
- Operating costs can be reduced because data communications can replace courier services and eliminate the need for meetings. Also, central data processing should be more economical.
- In larger systems with two or more computers, there can be a back-up data processing capacity: priority jobs can be routed to other computers if the main computer is busy, or if one computer fails.

Modes of Transmission There are two basic modes of transmission: *asynchronous* and *synchronous*.

Asynchronous Transmission In asynchronous transmission the characters are sent one by one with start and stop bits. This is suitable for sending data on standard telephone lines at slow speeds, e.g. using terminals where characters are sent at regular intervals.

Synchronous Transmission Synchronous transmission enables a stream of characters to be sent at a fixed rate. It is more efficient for transmitting large volumes of data at high speeds, e.g. data from a magnetic tape unit.

Rate of Data Transmission The rate of data transmission between computers and/or communication equipment or devices is measured in bits per second or by a system called the *baud rate*. To all intents and purposes, these can be taken as being the same.

Transmission Methods There are three basic methods of transmitting data over a communications link.

- *Simplex*;
- *Half-duplex*;
- *Full-duplex*.

Simplex Simplex is in one direction only and is rarely used.

Half-duplex Half-duplex is two-way but not at the same time.

Full-duplex Full-duplex is two-way and simultaneous, i.e. both ends can transmit and receive at the same time.

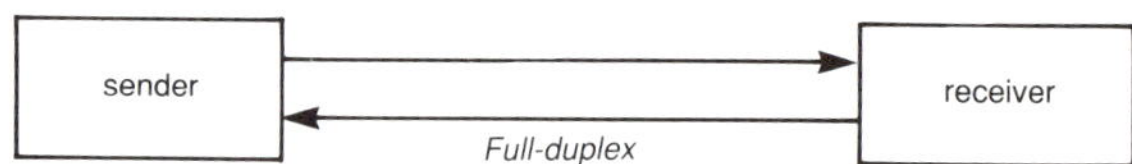

Electronic Funds Transfer (EFT) *Electronic funds transfer* is a special type of message service between the computers of banks and other financial institutions. These messages are all to do with financial transactions, mainly transferring sums of money from one account to another. The computers in these organisations are linked throughout the world by a computer network. There are central computers which act as exchanges in that they route messages to the computer to which they are addressed and store messages in transit if necessary. Many people have their salaries paid directly into their own bank accounts by the organisation for which they work; these payments are handled by this communications network.

EFT is becoming more widespread with the direct transfer of money from personal bank accounts to shops to pay for goods instead of using cheques.

The security of the system is very important, as it is essential to protect EFT from unauthorised interference.

Cash Card Terminals

The use of cash card terminals involves EFT. A message is sent from the cash card terminal to the bank's computer, and will include a check on the bank card validity, the personal identification number (PIN), and details of the cash to be withdrawn from a particular account.

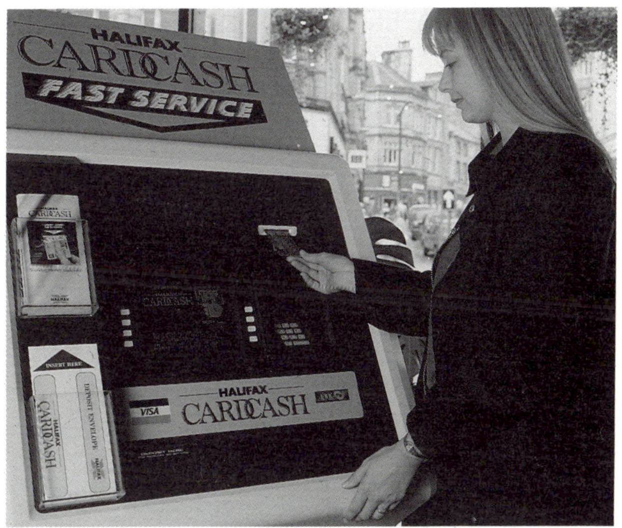

A cash card terminal

9 Software

Software *Software* is the term used to describe the programs (instructions) which enable a computer system to be used more easily.

Machine Code Originally, computers were programmed in *machine code*. This is a set of binary digits which can be decoded by the computer's control unit.

```
111 Ø1Ø ØØØ ØØØ
ØØ1 ØØØ ØØØ 1Ø1
ØØ1 ØØØ ØØØ 11Ø
ØØ1 ØØØ ØØØ 111
Ø11 ØØØ ØØ1 ØØØ
```

A snippet of machine code

Advantages:

- Machine code is economic in terms of memory requirements.
- Machine code programs are very quick to run as no translation is necessary.

Disadvantages:

- Programming in machine code is very slow and tedious.
- The programs are difficult to debug, i.e. to sort out any errors.

Assembly Languages *Assembly languages* were soon introduced. These made the writing of machine code programs easier. Instead of binary digits, sets of letters are used which are easy to remember. Each instruction of an assembly language generally translates into one machine code instruction.

```
EQU $ØØ8Ø
EQU $ØØ81
ORG $ØØ2Ø
LDA A DATA1
LDA B DATA2
STA A DATA2
STA B DATA1
SWI
```

A snippet of assembly language

Advantage:

- The letter codes are easier to remember and understand than the binary digits of machine code.

Disadvantages:

- An *assembler* (a translation program) is needed to translate the assembly program into machine code.
- This is expensive and takes up storage space.

High-level Languages

A *high-level language* is a computer language which is nearer to human language and is based on the problems being solved rather than on the computer being used.

Each instruction of a high-level language program translates into several machine-code instructions.

Advantages:

- High-level languages are more like 'English' for business applications, or more like mathematical notation for scientific applications, so these languages are easier to learn, write and understand.
- They are developed for use on more than one computer. Therefore it is possible to take a program written in a high-level language from one computer and use it on another.

Disadvantages:

- Although high-level languages are supposed to be portable from one machine to another, there are often different 'dialects' for different machines.
- High-level languages need to be translated into machine code.
- They are not as economical on memory and execution time as machine-code programs.

Examples of high-level languages are:

FORTRAN (FORmula TRANslation) – a scientific language;

ALGOL (ALGOrithmic Language) – used for scientific or mathematical problems;

COBOL (COmmon Business Oriented Language) – used in business applications;

A snippet of a COBOL program

```
      03 FILLER               PIC X(3) VALUE SPACES.
      03 WS-P-SURNAME         PIC X(12).
      03 FILLER               PIC X(5) VALUE SPACES.
      03 WS-P-AGE             PIC 99.

01  WS-EOF-FLAG               PIC XXX.
88  END-OF-EMPLOYEE-FILE     VALUE "YES".

PROCEDURE DIVISION.
MAIN-PROGRAM.
       PERFORM INITIALISATION.
       PERFORM HEADINGS.
       PERFORM PROCESS-EMPLOYEE-RECORD
               UNTIL END-OF-EMPLOYEE-FILE.
       PERFORM TERMINATION.
       STOP RUN.
```

BASIC (Beginners' All-purpose Symbolic Instruction Code) – used in teaching computers to beginners;

A snippet of a BASIC program

```
100 FOR loop = 1 TO 50
110 READ country$(loop), currency$(loop)
120 NEXT loop
130 PRINT
140 PRINT "COUNTRY"; TAB(15);"CURRENCY"
```

Pascal (named after the French mathematician Blaise Pascal) – used for teaching logical structured programming.

A snippet of a PASCAL program

```
PROGRAM Multiply(input,output);
 {a program that takes as input 2 integers and outputs
  their product}
VAR
      firstnumber   : integer
      secondnumber  : integer
      product       : integer
BEGIN
      WRITELN('Key in the first number');
      READLN(firstnumber);
      WRITELN('Key in the second number');
      READLN(secondnumber);
```

Fourth-generation Languages (4GLs) *4GLs* are user-oriented or query languages which have been developed to allow people with little or no training to write programs and access data. They closely resemble simple English.

They are used in organisations which require management information, e.g. local authorities and colleges, for massive record keeping and retrieval of information.

Translation Programs: Compilers and Interpreters Compilers and interpreters are large and complex programs which translate high-level programs into machine code.

Compilers A *compiler* takes a *source program* written in a high-level language and translates it into machine code. This is known as the *object program*. It is this object program which is then run.

Interpreters An *interpreter* translates a high-level program one line at a time whilst it is being run.

Advantages of a Compiler over an Interpreter Once the program is compiled it can be used again and again without being translated. Because of this running a compiled program is quicker than running one which is interpreted.

Advantages of an Interpreter over a Compiler When a program is being written or modified it can be more easily changed if the program is interpreted since the source program is always in the main memory.

Modular Programming *Modular programming* is a method by which large programs are divided up at the design stage into a number of small logical parts which can be treated as separate units.

Advantages:

- Each module is easier to specify, write and test.
- Changes in requirements can often be done by simple changes to existing modules or by adding new modules to the system.
- Some modules can be used by different programs, e.g. a date validation routine.

Programming Errors There are two types of programming errors: *compilation errors* and *run-time* errors.

Compilation Errors A compilation error is an error which is detected during the compilation of a program, that is, during its translation into machine code. These are *syntax errors*, i.e. errors in the use of the high-level language, such as in spelling or punctuation.

Run-time Errors A run-time error occurs in the execution of the program. The operating system may report difficulties in attempting to execute the program or may halt the execution of the program. Common causes of run-time errors are:

- a logical error, e.g. setting up a process which is to end at a certain condition, but it is never met so the program will try to run for ever;
- incorrect data, e.g. alphabetic data in a numeric field, causing problems when calculations are performed;
- incorrect instructions to the operating system, e.g. asking to load a file which does not exist.

Library Programs *Library programs* are small programs which perform a simple task. They are available to be used in other programs in the computer system, e.g. a sort routine or a calendar date validation routine. They are fully tested and properly documented.

Application Software *Application programs* are written to solve a particular problem. There are two types of application programs:

- user application programs;
- application packages.

User Application Programs User application programs are custom-built programs written, either by the user or by a software house, to perform a specific job, e.g. a stock-control program.

Application Packages *Application packages* are pre-written programs which may be purchased 'off-the-shelf' by the user. They are generalised programs for solving common business problems and can be run by a wide variety of users with few, if any, changes.

Application packages are available for routine applications such as word processing, financial modelling (spreadsheets), data management (record keeping) and payroll.

Application packages usually consist of:

- a program on disk or tape;
- documentation – which should include details on how to set up the package and how to use it, together with any technical information required for making amendments.

Advantages:

- Application packages offer cost savings on programming.
- They are tried and tested.
- They are often 'user friendly' and easy to run.

Disadvantages:

- They may not be exactly what is required by individual users.
- Documentation may be poor.

Integrated Software

Integrated software incorporates several applications packages into one, such as data management, word processing and financial modelling, or allows information generated in one package to be transferred to another.

Generic/Content-free Packages

Generic or *content-free packages* are those which have been produced to perform a specific task, such as word processing, spreadsheets or record keeping, where the user supplies the 'contents'.

Computer-aided Design (CAD)

Computers are used to design components and systems of mechanical, electrical and electronic devices. Precise drawings are produced by CAD, and the design may be investigated and altered with the use of powerful computers.

CAD is used in designing vehicles and vehicle components, ships, buildings, machine components and electrical circuits.

Computer-aided Manufacture (CAM)

Computers are used in manufacturing industries in the form of:

- industrial robots;

- Computer Numerical Control (CNC) of machine tools;
- integrated CAD/CAM;
- automated handling of materials.

Computer-assisted Learning (CAL) CAL refers to teaching packages written for use on a computer. They consist of interactive programs, often using sound, colour and graphics, which allow the computer to respond to the input made by the student, and give feedback on the success level of the student.

Computer Simulations *Computer simulations* are used to provide a mathematical model of a changing situation. The interaction of various inputs into a situation are modelled to allow the user to study the effect of various combinations of factors without having to build or study the real thing. They allow the user to investigate a situation without being exposed to the possible dangers of that situation.

Simulations may be done on changing physical situations and are used in the design of such things as bridges, buildings and cars.

They may also be done for changes in financial, social and political situations and may be used to attempt to predict future events.

A simulation is limited to the understanding of the designers of the simulation.

Operating Systems The *operating system* is the software which controls the overall operation of a computer. It is a suite of programs which co-ordinates all the components of the computer. Its purpose is to provide a background in which users' programs are run, to make sure that the best use is made of computing resources, and to keep to a minimum the amount of intervention necessary from operators. It provides communication between the computer and the person operating it. It can be thought of as a master program which directs other programs to do the jobs required.

The operating system is usually kept in a backing store, being loaded into the main memory as the computer is switched on. When the computer is running, some parts of the operating system will be in the main memory all the time, while other routines will be loaded only when required.

Functions of the Operating System

The functions of the operating system are to:

- control the overall operation of the computer system;
- schedule jobs to provide continuous processing;
- control the use of peripherals for input and output;
- call programs and data into main storage as required;
- detect and report any faults, e.g. malfunctioning peripherals;
- protect the programs and data of the various users from being corrupted by each other;
- keep a log of the use of the computer;
- communicate with the computer operator.

Bootstrap (Boot Program)

A *bootstrap* is a loading program which is used at the start of each day. It is usually permanently in ROM. It allows the operating system and programs to be loaded into the computer's memory.

A' bootstrap' program is so called because it is as if the computer is lifting itself up by its own bootstraps

Supervisor

A *supervisor* is the main component of an operating system. It is a program which organises the use of the hardware for the programs being run. It keeps track of the programs that are being run and the peripherals and files that these programs need.

Scheduler A *scheduler* is a program which organises the timetable of the CPU. It decides which programs may use the CPU at any time. Some programs may be given a greater priority and the scheduler is responsible for ensuring that the programs with the highest priority are given more time.

Utility Programs A *utility program* is one which performs a single simple routine task, e.g.:

sorting files;
merging files;
making copies of files and programs;
listing the content of magnetic tapes;
transferring data files from magnetic tape to disk;
transferring the contents of a VDU screen to a printer.

Editor An *editor* is a utility program which is used to create and make alterations to files, data and programs.

Database Management System (DBMS) A *database management system* is a program package which has a general set of programs for managing a database (see page 90). It helps the user to set up, maintain, access and protect the database by separating it from the applications programs. The DBMS allows a user to access the database without being concerned with how the data is stored.

10 Program Design – Algorithms and Flowcharts

Algorithms An *algorithm* is an ordered list of instructions which gives the sequence of operations needed for solving a problem.

Program Design A variety of styles of algorithm is used for producing program designs. These include:
JSP (Jackson Structured Programming);
pseudocode;
flowcharts.

JSP (Jackson Structured Programming) JSP consists of structure charts which divide the program up into modules.

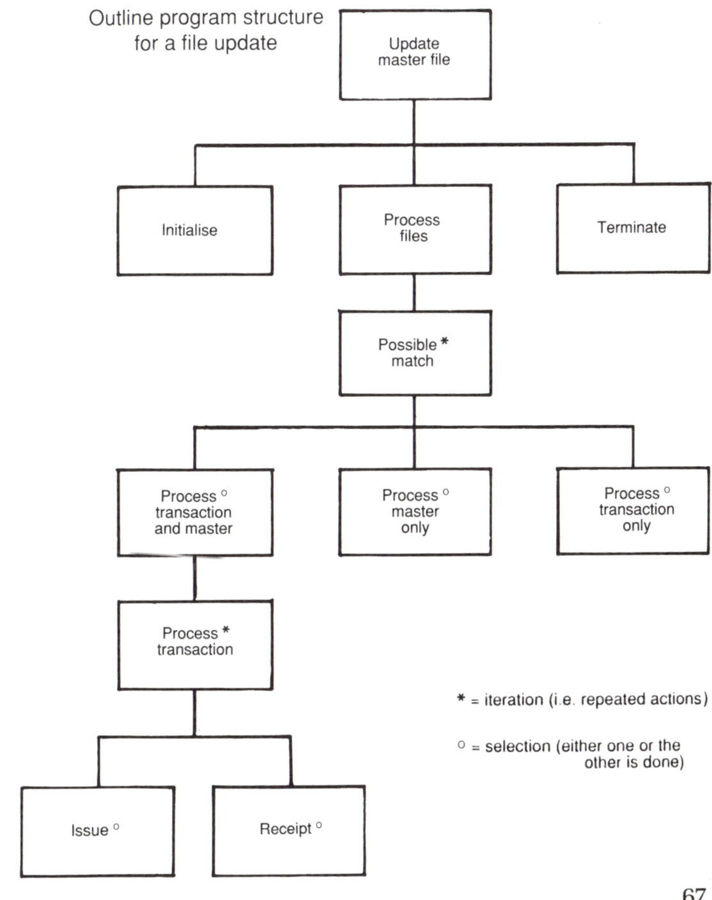

Pseudocode The set of instructions is written in a form resembling ordinary English.

```
while not end of file
    process record
    add one to record count
    read next record
end while
```

An example of pseudocode

Flowcharts A *flowchart* is a diagram representing a sequence of operations.

Flowcharts consist of:

- symbols (there are several standard shapes);
- messages written inside the symbols;
- lines connecting the symbols to show the order of operations;
- annotations, i.e. further explanations given in the margin.

There are two types of flowchart: *program flowcharts* and *systems flowcharts*.

Program Flowcharts Program flowcharts are used to show the order and logic of a computer program. They can be divided into:

- outline program flowcharts;
- detailed program flowcharts.

Program Flowchart Symbols The symbols used in program flowcharts are as follows:

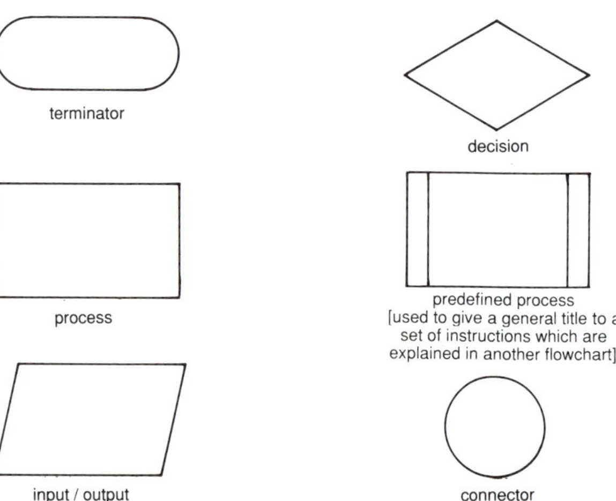

Outline Program Flowcharts

An outline program flowchart shows:

- the start and end of the program;
- the input/output operations;
- how the data is processed;
- the main sections of the program.

They should be written using ordinary human language, e.g. English, avoiding language which is too close to a particular programming language or computer.

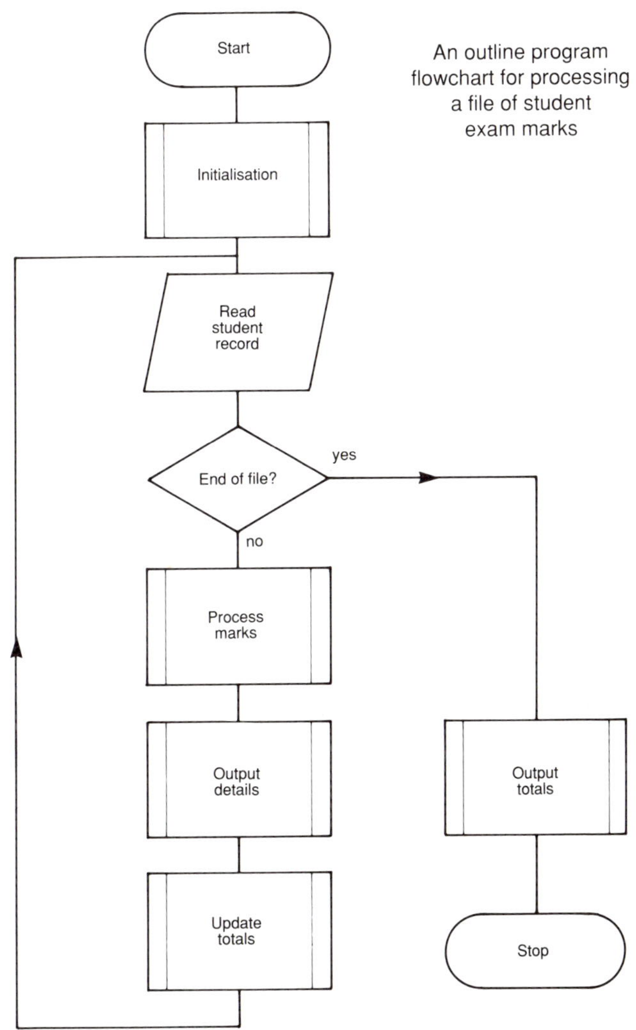

An outline program flowchart for processing a file of student exam marks

Detailed Program Flowcharts

A detailed program flowchart shows all the operations carried out by a program step by step. It should be sufficiently detailed for the program code to be written directly from it.

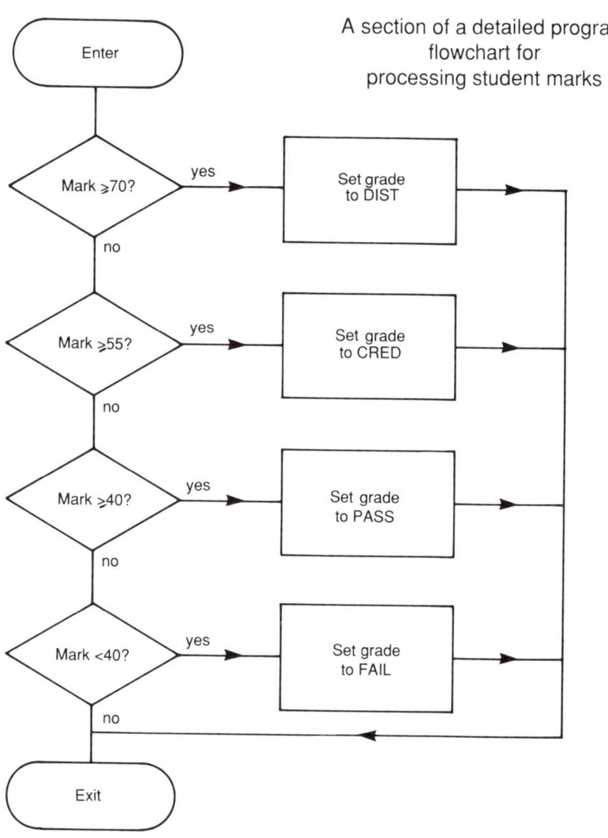

A section of a detailed program flowchart for processing student marks

Systems Flowcharts

Systems flowcharts are used to show the stages involved in the overall computer system. This includes the description of:

- inputs to the system, including the collection and preparation of data;
- computer operations, e.g. calculations, sorts and updates;
- the backing store files used, including the type of backing storage;

- outputs from the system, e.g. the reports produced;
- manual and clerical operations.

Systems Flowchart Symbols Many symbols are used in systems flowcharts, and the main ones are shown below.

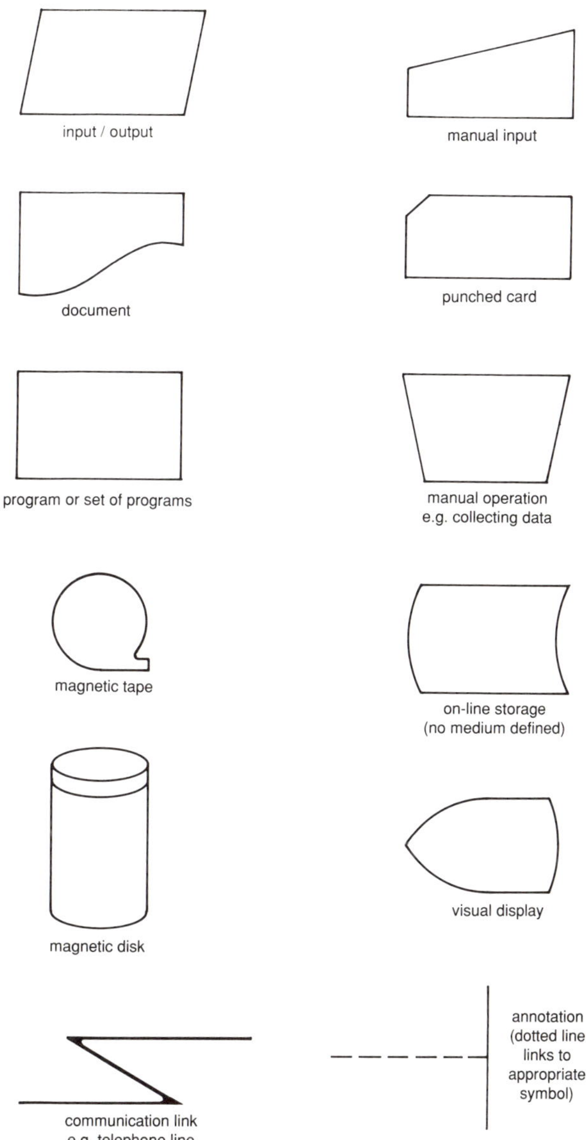

An Example of a System Flowchart

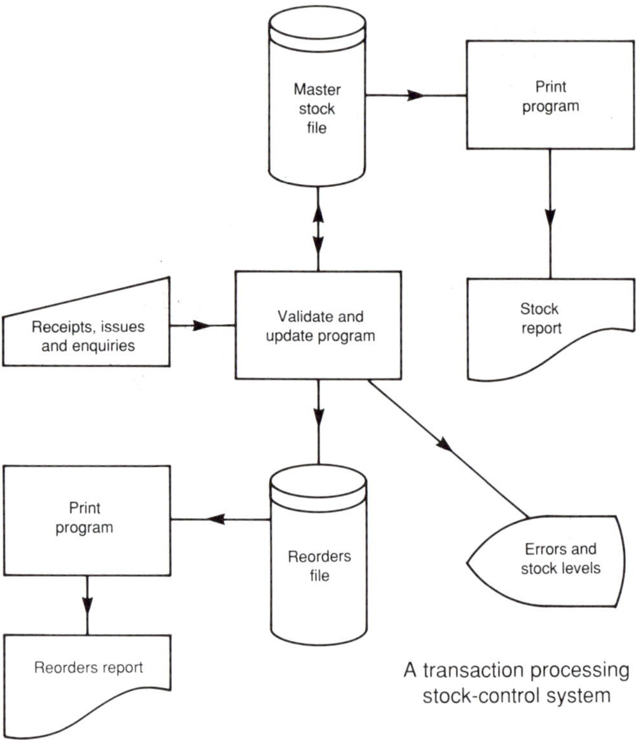

A transaction processing stock-control system

Trace Tables

A *trace table* can be used to dry run a program, i.e. to check it using pencil and paper before trying it out on a computer.

The values of all the different inputs, expected results of calculations and all the outputs are noted down.

A completed trace table is a very useful aid when trying to debug a program, i.e. sort out the errors.

Worked Example

A set of marks for 6 students are stored in an array, i.e. a list called mark (counter).

The contents of this array are shown below.

mark (counter)

counter	1	2	3	4	5	6
marks	5	10	15	20	18	10

This flowchart shows the steps in the processing of these marks.
Complete the trace table for the flowchart.

Trace table

counter	mark	total	output

You have to use the data supplied, i.e. the marks in the array, and work through the flowchart, writing down any changes in the values of counter, total, mark and output as they occur.

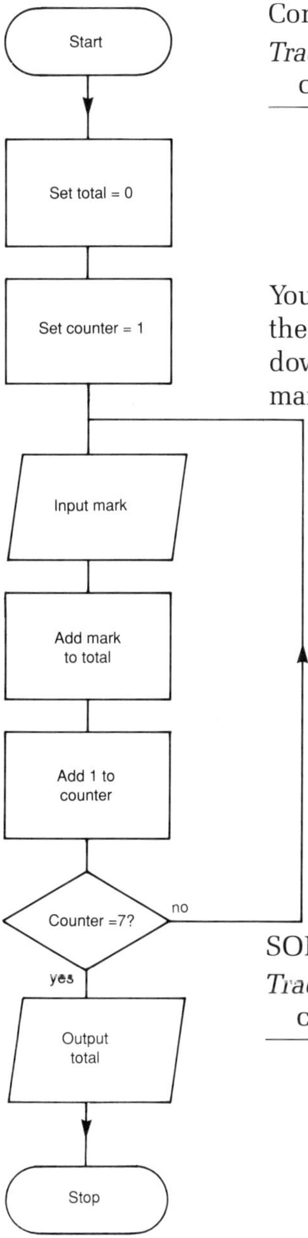

Start

Set total = 0

Set counter = 1

Input mark

Add mark to total

Add 1 to counter

Counter =7?

no

yes

Output total

Stop

A flowchart for adding student marks

SOLUTION

Trace table

counter	mark	total	output
1		0	–
1	5	5	–
2	10	15	–
3	15	30	–
4	20	50	–
5	18	68	–
6	10	78	–
7	–	–	78

11 Data Processing

Data Processing *Data processing* is the production of meaningful information from raw data.

The Difference between Data and Information Data of itself has no meaning.
e.g. 170192, 180293
The above becomes information when you are given some structure.
e.g. first two digits – day;
second two digits – month;
third two digits – year;
so 170192 becomes: 17th January 1992,
and 180293 becomes: 18th February 1993.

Organisation of Data Data needs to be organised and the first step is to organise it into *files*.

File Structure

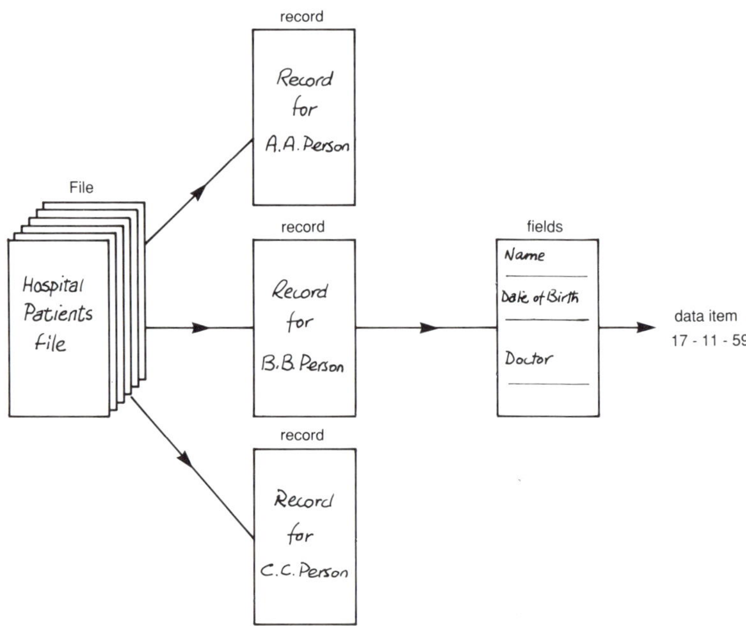

File A *file* is a collection of records on a related topic, e.g. a Hospital Patients File is a collection of Hospital Patients Records.

Record A *record* is a collection of related data which refer to the same event, person or object, arranged with some structure, usually into fields, e.g. each hospital patient's record refers to one particular patient.

Field Within each *field* of a record is a *data item* made up of one or more characters, e.g. each hospital patient's record will be divided into fields such as Surname, Date of Birth, etc. Each of these will contain an item of data, e.g. the Surname Field could contain JONES. Fields may be of fixed or variable length.

Key Field A *key field* is a particular field which holds a unique item of data used to identify the record, e.g. Hospital Patient Admission Number Field would contain a different number for each patient.

Fixed Length Fields Each field is given a predetermined length,
e.g. surname................................12 characters
first name ....8 characters
age ....3 digits

Advantages:

- Allocation of storage space is straightforward as each record takes up the same amount of space.
- Updating of files is simpler as each record takes up the same amount of space.
- Searching by computer is quicker.

Disadvantages:

- If not every part of each field is required, an unnecessary amount of space is wasted.

Variable Length Fields Each field is exactly the length required to hold the data.

Advantages:

- There is no wastage of storage space.
- There is no loss of data due to the field size being too small.

Disadvantages:

- The processing of the records is harder as end-of-field markers (data terminators) have to be set.

Data Terminator A *data terminator* is an extra piece of data which indicates when the end of a variable-length field has been reached.

Pointer A *pointer* is an item of data which is used to hold the location of further data. It can be thought of as an arrow. Pointers are used in data structures to provide the links between related records.

Master File A *master file* is the current up-to-date reference file which is the principal source of information on a particular subject. It can be updated or amended as necessary.

Transaction File A *transaction file* is a collection of records in a temporary file which is used to update the master file.

Batch Processing *Batch processing* was traditionally the only system used for data processing. There was no other way processing could be done, since the backing storage available (paper tape, punched cards and magnetic tape) allowed only serial access to files (i.e. starting at the beginning of the file and working through in one direction). The system lends itself to situations where all transactions are collected together and submitted to the computer in a batch, and is still used for payroll, gas and electricity billing, etc.

Advantages:

- There is no need for the user to be present.
- Preparation and operation is done by skilled staff.
- As there is a high utilisation of the machine, batch processing is efficient.

Disadvantages:

- Information may be out of date because of the time taken in collecting, verifying and validating the data and then running the update program.
- The user cannot intervene during the run.
- Batch processing requires an expensive computer and a large staff.
- The amount of work is variable, so there may be staffing problems.

A Systems Flowchart for a Typical Batch Processing System

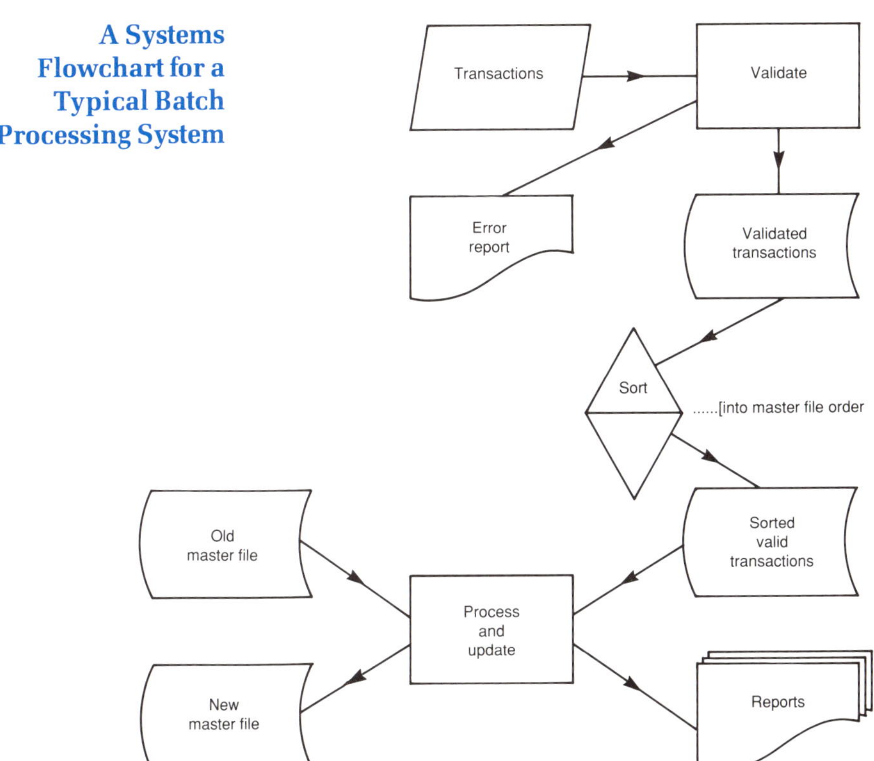

Hit Rate Batch processing is used when the *hit rate* is high, i.e. when all, or nearly all, the records in the master file need to be updated.

Sequence of Events for Batch Processing There are four stages in the sequence of events that takes place in a batch processing system:

1. Assemble the Transaction Data All the transaction data is collected together and either converted into machine-readable input, or is input directly using machine-readable documents, e.g. turnaround documents (see page 29).

2. Validate the Transaction Data All the transaction data must be validated, i.e. checked to see if the data fulfils a certain set of criteria. This is done by a validation program which will filter out all the unreasonable transactions.

Transactions which have been rejected are corrected manually, then resubmitted to the validation program.

A correct, valid batch of transactions is produced, called a transaction file.

3. Sort the Transaction File The transaction file is sorted into the same sequence as the master file so that the two files are now both sequential files. This is necessary because, in this type of processing, the files can be processed only by starting at the beginning and working through record by record, in one direction.

4. Update and Produce a New Master File The master file will compare the transaction records on the transaction file with those on the master file, process the amendments, and produce a *new* updated master file. Every record on the old master file must be carried on to the new master file even if the record is not updated.

Transaction Processing

In *transaction processing*, data is used to update the master file as and when the transactions occur. Enquiries can also be made of the master file at any time, with an immediate response.

Transaction processing is used when the hit rate is low, i.e. when only a small number of records on the master file needs to be updated.

Examples of use include: airline booking systems, hotel and theatre booking systems.

A systems flowchart for a typical transaction processing system

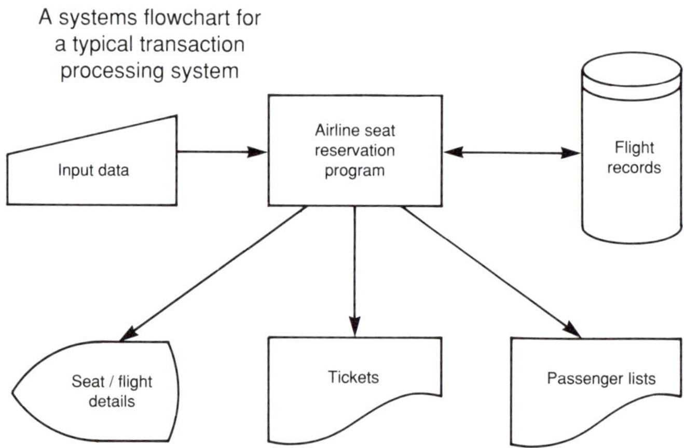

Magnetic Tape Labels There are two types of magnetic tape label:

- external and
- internal.

External Label An *external label* is simply a piece of gummed paper stuck to the tape reel cover or collar. The operator will write on this such information as:

- the reel number;
- the name of the file;
- the date the file was created;
- the retention period.

This label is used by the operator to identify the data on the tape.

Internal Label An *internal label* is written on to by the operating system of the computer. There are two types of internal label:

- header labels and
- trailer labels.

Header Labels *Header labels* are written at the beginning of a file. They serve to identify the contents of the file, and usually contain most or all of the following information:

- the name of the file, e.g. ACCOUNT (name or number);
- the reel sequence number, vital if there are two or more reels to the file (*multi-reel files*);
- the version number of the file, as in grandfather, father, son (see page 88);
- the creation date;
- the purge or expiry date (a security feature indicating the earliest date on which the tape can be overwritten).

Trailer Labels *Trailer labels* are written at the end of the file. They contain some of the information that was in the header label, such as:

- file name;
- reel sequence number;
- version number.

In addition, trailer labels provide a *block count* (which indicates the number of blocks of data which were originally written to the file), and a *continuation indicator* (used to indicate whether or not a further reel follows the present reel.

How the Tape Labels are Used

The operator checks the external label to determine which tape(s) is to be used for the job.

The *supervisor* (part of the operating system) is informed of the name of the file, the reel sequence number and the version number by the operator via the *job control language*, which is a special language use to identify a job and describe its requirements to the operating system.

The operating system reads the header label and checks that this matches the information given. Any discrepancies are signalled so that the operator can take action.

As the file is read, the supervisor counts the number of blocks read and checks this against the block count in the trailer label. Any discrepancies are reported. This is a check that no data has been lost.

If the file is being written to, on opening the file the purge date is checked against the run date and the operator alerted if an error has occurred.

Data Validation

Data validation is the checking of raw input for errors before it is processed.

Validation is performed by a program in order to check that the data is sensible, accurate, complete and reasonable.

It is essential that as many errors as possible are detected before the input data is processed. The inputting of wrong data may cause a program to stop.

Wrong data cannot be corrected by a program and it is often expensive to find where the mistake is afterwards.

Validation Techniques

Several techniques may be used to ensure that any data input is valid.

Format Check

A *format check* ensures that data is of the correct type and order, e.g. ABC123456, 3 characters followed by 6 digits, a check is done to see that this is obtained.

Range Check A *range check* ensures that the data falls within the correct range, e.g.

Age – no more than 3 digits allowed.

Valid account number of 6 digits, so if less than or equal to 99 999 or more than or equal to 1 000 000 the number is not correct.

Check Digits *Check digits* are used for International Standard Book Numbers and many account numbers. They are used to make sure that the individual digits in the number input are in the correct order.

A common error is to transpose digits when writing them down or keying them in e.g. 12*43*5 instead of 12*34*5.

A series of arithmetic operations is done on a number which results in the production of a check digit. This extra digit (or letter) is added to the end of the number code and becomes part of the code. When the account number is entered into the computer, the same formula is applied to the number and if the recalculated digit matches the one entered on the code then the code number has been entered correctly.

Consistency Check This is a check to ensure that the data which is input in one place is consistent with that input in another, e.g. if the input of title is 'MR', then sex should be entered as male, not female.

Hash Total A *hash total* is a total figure of all the items of data being input, such as employee numbers. The hash total calculated by the computer should be the same as that calculated manually before the data is input. If a figure is missing, the hash total will not balance. Hash totals check that *all* the data has been transmitted correctly.

Batch Totals Where many transaction records enter a batch-processing system, it is usual to divide them into batches, each one with its own batch control record. A count will be done by the computer on the number of transactions processed, and this will be checked against the batch control record.

Control Totals *Control totals* are used in a batch-processing system. They are the subtotals for each batch, e.g. in a batch which has transactions for different departments, a count can be made for the number of transactions in each department as transaction records are created. Control records are written containing these subtotals. A count is done by the computer as the batch is being processed and the total number processed should match the numbers input.

Test Data *Test data* is sample data which has been chosen carefully to test a program fully. It is used to check the accuracy of the processing and to check that the program works according to the design specification.

Test data should be chosen to ensure that:

- every program statement is executed at least once;
- every route through the program is tested;
- every error routine is tested.

Test data consists of three categories:

- *normal data*
- *extreme data*
- *illegal data*.

Normal Data Normal data includes the general data that the program was designed to handle.

Extreme Data Extreme data includes valid data at the upper and lower limits of acceptability, e.g. for numeric data this would include the use of very large or very small numbers. For a file processing program the test file could contain just a single record.

Illegal Data Illegal data includes invalid data that the program should reject. It is used to test that the program is capable of rejecting this data rather than trying to process it.

Steps in the System Life Cycle

1. Problem Definition
2. Feasibility Study
3. Analysis
4. System Design
5. Implementation
6. Maintenance

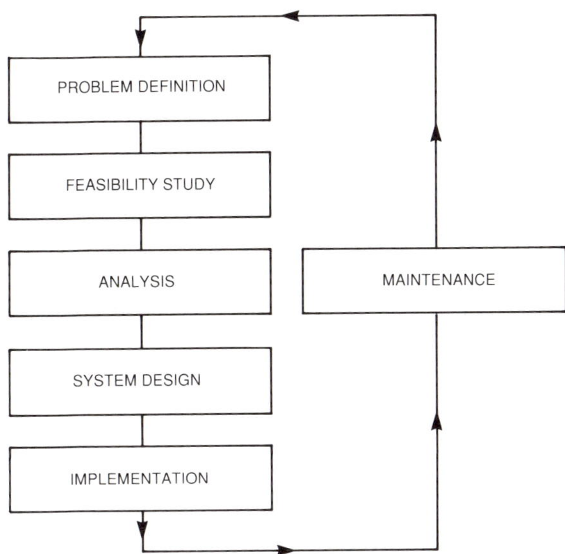

1. Problem Definition The problem definition is a written statement of the scope of the problem. It is based on studies which include interviews with management and current and future users.

2. Feasibility Study A feasibility study is an investigation into whether there is a practical solution to the problem. It will include an estimate of the cost and benefits of the system. Many projects do not go beyond this stage.

3. Analysis Analysis is the logical process which examines what must be done to solve the problem. It involves a careful consideration of all the data and development of all the necessary algorithms (set of rules used in problem-solving).

4. System Design System design is concerned with how the problem is to be solved in detail and includes such things as:

necessary programs;
data capture;
file design;
report layouts;
hardware specifications;
necessary procedures;
implementation schedules.

5. Implementation

New hardware is selected, ordered and installed.
Programs are coded, debugged and documented.
Operating procedures are developed.
Security and auditing procedures are worked out.
A formal test plan is prepared.
A staff training plan is prepared.
Backup procedures are worked out.
Implementation could be either 'going live' on a certain date or a parallel run of both computer and manual systems, checking output from both for a set period of time.

6. Maintenance

Maintenance is on-going with any computer system. Continuing support is needed to keep the system functioning at an acceptable level, as little bugs always slip through the system test.

Hardware will need to be upgraded over a period of time because of improvements in the technology available.

Changes in user requirements will necessitate changes in the system.

Documentation

Documentation consists of a set of notes and diagrams which describe the working of a program and its use. It is designed to help with the implementation and maintenance of the program.

Reasons for Producing Documentation

The reasons for producing documentation are:

- to enable the people designing and writing the program to work together;
- to show the program user what to do;
- to help the people responsible for maintaining and modifying the program.

Documentation can be divided into two types:

- documentation to help the programmer;
- documentation to help the user.

Documentation for the Programmer

Documentation for the programmer can be divided into systems documentation and program documentation.

Systems Documentation

Systems documentation is a carefully written set of specifications which include:

- processing procedures;
- sample input layouts;
- sample output layouts.

Program Documentation

Program documentation should include:

- a description of the problem;
- a program synopsis to describe briefly the various tasks;
- the files used, and their interdependence;
- structure charts;
- systems flowcharts;
- program flowcharts;
- program listing;
- operating instructions on how to run the program;
- a test plan and test data to check the program for accuracy.

All stages of a program should be carefully documented as this will enable:

- revision of the program should it be necessary because of external changes, e.g. new tax rates;
- revision if the organisation structure should change.

This documentation is essential so that the revisions can be made easily and efficiently. The documentation acts as a manual for program maintenance.

Documentation for the User

Documentation for the user should include the following:

- An explanation of the background of the system that the program is designed to work within.
- What the program does:
  - the problems the program solves;
  - the options it offers the user;
  - the limitations of the program, i.e. what it will not do.
- Computing requirements, i.e. the hardware and software necessary to run the program successfully.

- How to collect and prepare data for the program. If this involves special documents, there will be instructions on how to fill them in.
- How to operate the program, e.g. if the program is interactive (two-way) the details of the 'conversations' will be included.
- Details of error messages.
- How to interpret the output.

Security of Files Files may be in danger from three potential threats.

- They could be physically destroyed, e.g. by fire or floods, or by hardware failure such as a read/write head crash on to a disk, or scratches on a disk due to dust.
- They could be modified (changed), e.g. by being written over unintentionally, or by being updated with incorrect data for malicious reasons, such as fraud.
- They could be accessed by unauthorised people.

Methods of Protecting Data There are physical safeguards and software safeguards.

Physical Safeguards

- To safeguard against fire or theft, important files (or backups) are often kept in a separate building from the computer in a safe. Large organisations often have a fireproof room to protect their files.
- *Write-permit rings* are used. These are circles of plastic which can be inserted into the back of

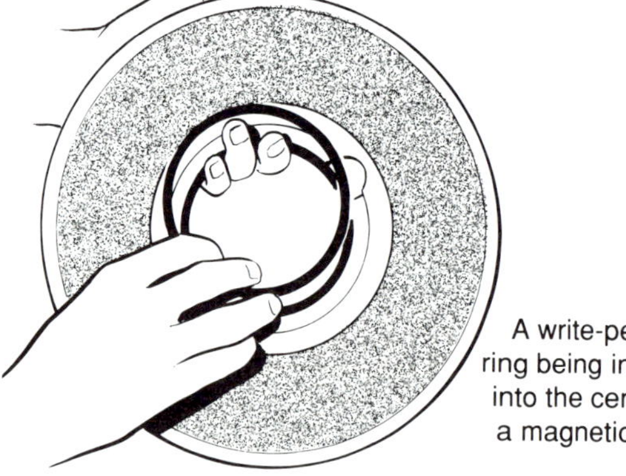

A write-permit ring being inserted into the centre of a magnetic tape

a reel of magnetic tape. If the ring is not present, data can be read from the tape but cannot be written to the tape, hence the phrase 'No ring no write'. In order to protect the data on the tapes, magnetic tape reels have these write-permit rings removed after use and are stored without them.

- Only authorised personnel may be allowed in certain areas in many computer installations to avoid unauthorised access to data.

Software Safeguards

Data may also be protected by software safeguards.

Using the Operating System

The computer's operating system can be used to maintain security. This can be done in three ways:

- using passwords;
- producing a log;
- producing audit trails.

Using Passwords

Anyone using the computer will be issued with a personal password in order to log on (enter into) and use the system.

Certain parts of the system and certain files may only be available to authorised personnel with passwords for these sections or these files.

Logs

The operating system can produce a *log*, i.e. a diary of all the events which have taken place on the computer: the users who have logged on, the programs that have been run and by whom and for how long, and any actions which have been taken by the operating system.

Audit Trails An *audit trail* can be made using the operating system for financial and accounting applications. In these individual transactions can be traced step-by-step through the computer system to ensure that nothing fraudulent has taken place.

Keeping Copies Data can be protected from destruction or modification by keeping copies. This can be done by keeping generations of files and by the periodic dumping of files on to backing storage. Care must be taken that keeping copies does not make unauthorised access easier.

Dumping *Dumping* is a safeguard against the loss of data by making backup copies of operational files from time to time. In a transaction processing system, 'dump' files are made at regular intervals, e.g. once every two hours. This is done by copying all the transaction data since the last backup. If the current data is lost for some reason, the up-to-date files can be recreated.

Generations of Files When a file is updated, the new file is called a *son*, the previous master file, from which it was produced, is called a *father* and the one before that

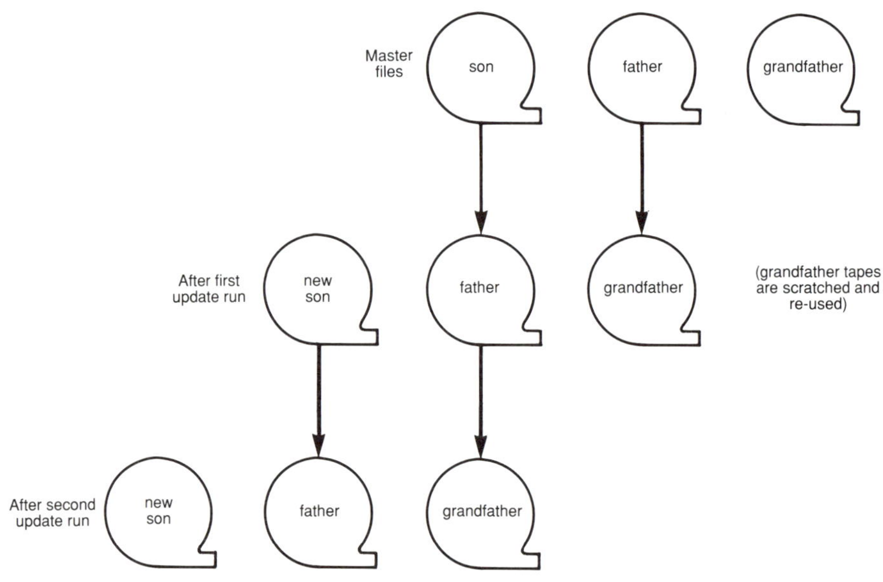

becomes a *grandfather*. When a son becomes a father, the father becomes a grandfather. Usually, three generations of a file are kept (grandfather, father, son) so that if data is lost or incorrectly updated it can be recovered.

12 Data Banks and Data Protection

Databases A *database* is a collection of files held on a computer system. The data in these files is so organised as to allow access to it by users in various ways.

Data Bank A *data bank* is a vast collection of files or databases, held on a computer system which allows direct access to the data for a large number of users by means of remote terminals.

Advantages of Data Banks

- Information occupies less space than traditional paper-based systems.
- Access to specific records is easy and very fast.
- Updating is a rapid, straightforward process.

Organisations which have Data Banks The Government:

Inland Revenue
The Registry of Births/Deaths
Department of Health and Social Security
National Health Service
The Driver and Vehicle Licensing Centre (DVLC) in Swansea
The Police

Banks
Insurance Companies
Credit Data Companies (record of creditworthiness)

Information Stored in Data Banks The actual data stored will vary from organisation to organisation. It will usually include such items as:

full name
date of birth
address
sex.

Then, depending on the organisation, such items as:

national insurance number
income tax code
employment details
pension details
vehicle details
details of loans
matrimonial details

family details
health details
details of criminal convictions.

Viewdata Systems *Viewdata systems* are two-way systems for transmitting requested text or graphics stored in computer databases via a telephone network for display on a TV screen. They are designed for a large number of uses and are meant to be cheap, easy to use and flexible.

Teletext *Teletext* is a computer-based information retrieval system which uses screen messages, either broadcast by television – for example the BBC system Ceefax or the ITV system Oracle – or provided interactively, e.g. British Telecom's Prestel.

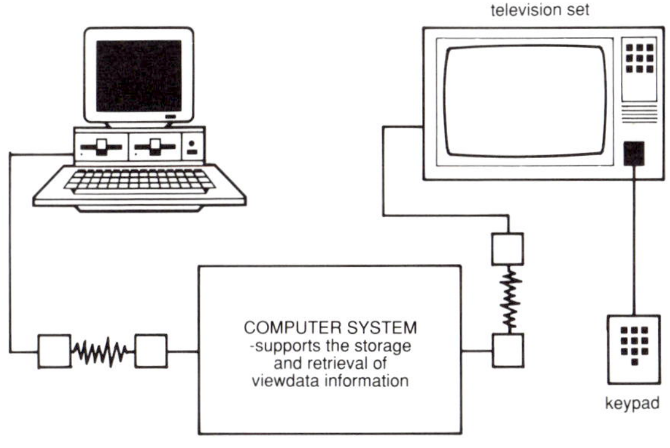

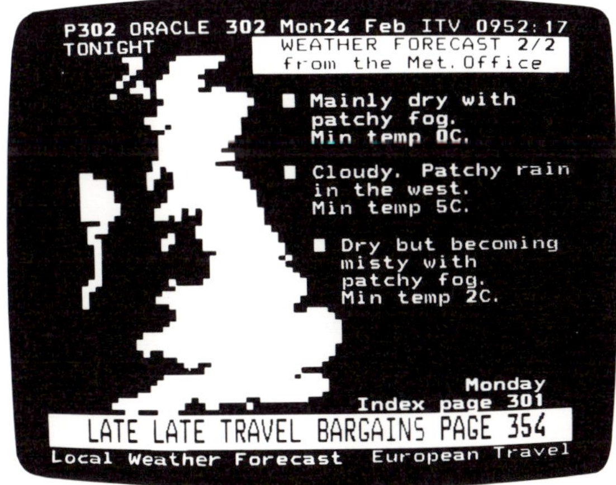

Prestel

Prestel is the best known public viewdata system. Run by British Telecom, it allows both commercial and private users to store and retrieve information from a computer via a telephone line. Over 320 000 pages of information are stored on 6 large computers in different parts of the country. Information is available 24 hours per day.

Information can be updated by the minute and ranges from the general, e.g. weather, news, sports results, to the specialised, e.g. share prices, local leisure facilities.

The user links in to Prestel via the telephone system, with an adapted television set, a specialised viewdata terminal, or a microcomputer. If a micro is used, it is linked to the telephone via a modem which adapts the telephone signal into a form which the micro can understand.

The system is interactive, and all users can make bookings, send messages and request information. Having logged on to Prestel the user can go straight to any page by keying in the page number, or if this is not known, the user is routed through a series of index menus.

The Cost of Prestel

Prestel is not free, the costs include:

- the TV, telephone or computer adaptor;
- an annual subscription;
- a charge for the telephone link;
- charges for some of the frames of information.

Data Protection Act 1984

The Data Protection Act 1984 gives individuals the right of access to personal data, and it regulates the holding and use of such data. With limited exceptions, the Act requires the registration of all those who control the contents and use of automatically processed personal data. The Data Protection Act covers only computerised records – it does not cover paper-based files.

The Act sets out principles of data protection, which require personal data to be:

- obtained fairly and lawfully;

- held only for the lawful purposes specified in the register entry;
- used or disclosed only in accordance with the data user's register entry;
- adequate, relevant and not excessive for the purpose;
- made available to data subjects on request;
- accurate and, where necessary, kept up to date;
- held no longer than is necessary;
- properly protected against loss or disclosure.

Individuals have a right to be informed about whether personal data is held on them and, where appropriate, to have this data corrected or deleted. However, the onus is not on data users to provide this information but on data subjects to request it.

Personal Data *Personal data* is information (recorded on a computer) about identifiable living individuals.

Data Subject A *data subject* is an individual to whom personal data relates.

Data User A *data user* is an individual or organisation controlling the use and content of personal data processed automatically.

Data Protection Register The Data Protection Register is maintained by the Data Protection Registrar to record details of declarations made by data users as required by the Data Protection Act 1984.

Integrity of Data *Integrity of data* is the term used to describe the accuracy and correctness of data during and after processing. Data which has not been accidentally or maliciously corrupted is said to have integrity.

Mail Merging Mail merging is used for combining a standard document, such as a letter on a word-processing system, with a list of names and addresses, from a database for example, so that many letters are produced which appear personalised with the appropriate names and details inserted at certain points.

Electronic Mail *Electronic mail* is a service whereby a message is converted to electronic signals and sent from a data terminal via a telecommunications network. It can be classified as follows:

- telex (teleprinter exchange);
- facsimile (FAX);
- computer-based services.

Electronic mail is:

- an alternative to the ordinary mail service;
- a complement to the telephone;
- an alternative to travel for conferences and meetings.

Advantages:

- Electronic mail is rapid, reliable and convenient.
- It does not require the sender and the receiver to be present at the same time. Messages can be stored or forwarded and retrieved from any terminal.

Disadvantages:

- Electronic mail is expensive when compared with the ordinary mail service.
- As yet it is not widely available.
- International standards are still needed, i.e. methods of data transmission compatible between different systems.
- It is not easy to protect the data being transmitted from unauthorised access.

3 Computer Personnel and Computer Bureaux

Computer Personnel There are five main sections within a computer department, or data processing department.

- *Data Preparation*;
- *Data Control*;
- *Operations*;
- *Systems Analysis and Design*;
- *Programming* (*Systems* and *Applications*).

The boundaries between these can be variable, depending on the *size* of the data processing department, e.g. Programming and Analysis may be combined.

The person in charge of the department is called the *data processing manager* (DP Manager).

The Data Preparation, Data Control and Operations Sections contain the personnel involved in the day-to-day running of the processing department.

Systems Analysis, Systems Design and the Programming Sections are involved in creating new systems or programs to be run on the computer.

Data Preparation This section is responsible for converting raw data (source data) into machine-readable form. The data preparation operators are called:

key punch operators if the medium is punched card (outdated);

key to tape operators if the medium is magnetic tape;

key to disk operators if the medium is magnetic disk;

Verifying work will be done by a senior operator.

Data Control The Data Control Section is responsible for the accuracy of the information on the computer and for the procedures, which involve:

- collection of input data;
- preparation of the input data;
- initial checking of the input data;
- balancing and filing of control totals;
- circulation of the computer output.

Operations

Computer operators are responsible for the day-to-day running of the computer. The type of work depends on the size of the computer installation and the type of operating system used. Certain jobs are common to most situations.

Operating the computer equipment involves:

- mounting magnetic tapes or disk packs;
- moving magnetic tapes or disk packs to and from storage;
- watching the operator's console for program instructions or operating system instructions;
- monitoring a program as it is running;
- placing special stationery in line printers;
- noting the amount of stationery and computer time used in order to charge the appropriate department;
- making sure the line printer does not run out of paper;
- ensuring that only permitted personnel are allowed into the computer room;
- being responsible for correct behaviour in the computer room – no smoking, eating or drinking;
- keeping the machine room tidy;
- possibly cleaning the machines or machine room.

Someone in the Operations Section (usually the File Librarian) will be responsible for the security of magnetic tapes or disks. They will inform the operator of the particular tapes or disks to be used in a particular job, whether write permit rings are required, and so give permission for data to be overwritten.

A senior operator, or the operations manager, will schedule the jobs. He or she will be responsible for deciding the priority order of jobs to be run.

Systems Analysis and Design

A *systems analyst* is responsible for analysing a system and designing a new one, including deciding whether or not the system requires a computer solution.

Programming There are two types of programmer:

- *system programmers*;
- *applications programmers*.

System Programmers System programmers are concerned with writing programs for a particular computer operating system, developing new program languages and developing or improving compilers. They usually write in low-level languages.

Applications Programmers Applications programmers are responsible for the planning, writing, testing and documenting of programs which have a particular application, e.g. sales analysis, payroll, invoicing, analysing the results of a scientific experiment. They usually write in high-level languages.

The Organisation of a Large Data Processing Department

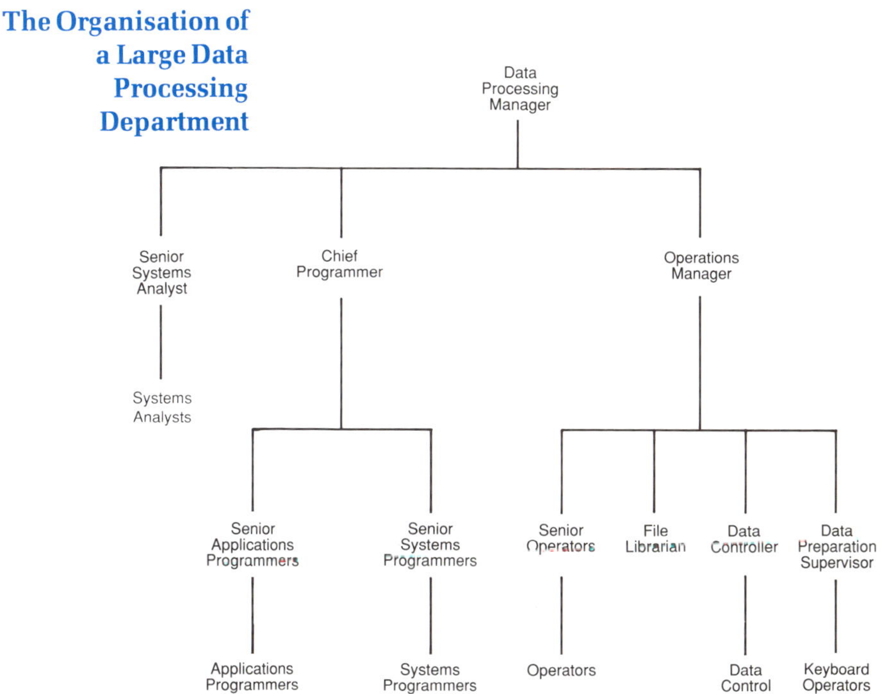

Computer Bureaux Computer bureaux offer independent sources of computing facilities in terms of both hardware and software. These services may be hired to perform required jobs. A variety of services is offered including:

- data preparation;
- computer time;
- program packages of common applications;
- systems analysis;
- systems design;
- programming;
- consultancy.

Computer bureaux may be used by organisations which require computer facilities but cannot afford their own. They may also be used by organisations which have the facilities but use the bureaux at busy times or peak periods when in-house facilities are overstretched, when specialist equipment is needed, for advice on purchasing software, or when there is no appropriate in-house expertise on a certain topic.

4 Computers and Society

Computers and Society Most people think that computers and related technologies have brought great social changes and will continue to do so. Not everyone is in agreement as to what future changes will be, the rate at which they will occur, and to what extent they will be for the benefit of society.

Benefits of Computers The benefits of computers could be said to include:

- greater efficiency;
- increased productivity;
- cleaner and safer working conditions;
- shorter working hours;
- more leisure time.

Drawbacks of Computers The drawbacks of computers could be said to include:

- loss of jobs for some due to greater efficiency of computers in some types of work;
- invasion of personal privacy as vast amounts of personal data can be stored and accessed with ease;
- unauthorised access to business data allowing an increased possibility of crime;
- people are divided into two groups – either computer-literate, or not.

The Effects of Computers on Employment There are two conflicting views on the impact of computers:

1. the computer will throw millions out of work;
2. the computer will create wealth, which in turn will provide the spending power to generate new service, leisure and education industries.

Computers Supplant Jobs In some situations, computers may replace people, and indeed have already done so. Therefore, the pattern of employment is changing. In factories, many shop-floor and production-line jobs are being replaced by robots and automated production lines. Clerical staff are being superseded by office automation.

Many of these tasks may be unskilled, dull and repetitive, and the people who do them may not find alternative employment without training or retraining for skilled jobs.

"Computers supplant jobs"

Computers Create Jobs The existence of computers leads directly to jobs being created for design, manufacture, sales and programming in the computer industry itself. Indirectly, other jobs result from the new, improved product applications of microelectronics. More people are now involved in information occupations than in manufacturing and agriculture.

"Computers create jobs"

Computer jobs often involve skilled and therefore better-paid people, but vacancies are fewer in number.

Some computer jobs, such as in data preparation and computer manufacturing, may be as boring as many other jobs.

Computers Alter Jobs When an organisation introduces computers, the power structure may change, often with the new people being appointed into key posts, e.g. as the information services manager.

Computerisation has led to changes in employment patterns and prospects. The following may result from computerisation:

- retraining;
- redeployment;
- de-skilling;
- changes in working practices;
- regrading of staff and changes in career prospects;
- redundancy;
- changes in working conditions.

Retraining Where possible, many organisations will choose to make full use of their existing staff. Depending on the nature of the job, the retraining may be extensive or quite a minor task. For example, a typist has keyboard skills which are readily transferable to the task of word-processing.

Redeployment Redeployment (i.e. moving staff from one area of work or responsibility to another, often with retraining) is a common result of computerisation, as it generally reduces the staffing requirement.

De-skilling Some jobs may be de-skilled by the use of computers, others not. For example, a wages clerk requires less skill when the job is computerised than when using a manual system, whereas a higher level of skill is needed to use a word processor than is needed to use a typewriter.

Changes in Working Practices As a result of computerisation, staff may be required to carry out a wider range of tasks than before.

Regrading and Career Prospects Improvements in job gradings are often introduced in order to encourage staff to accept computerisation. However, in many industries the career prospects have diminished, e.g. in the banking industry there are fewer managerial posts due to increased efficiency after computerisation.

Redundancy Computerisation of a job usually reduces staff requirements for the existing level of work. However, computerisation often occurs in response to the expansion of an organisation, so redundancies do not necessarily occur.

Changes in Working Conditions In offices, certain health risks may arise as a result of using a computer or related equipment, e.g. regular use of a VDU may result in eye strain, headaches and backache. Equipment and environments should therefore be designed to minimise the health hazards, e.g. by gentle lighting, lack of screen flicker, properly designed seating.

In industry, the supervision and servicing of computerised machinery is generally a cleaner, safer job than with other types of machinery.

List of Abbreviations

4GL	Fourth Generation Language
ADC	analogue-to-digital converter
ALU	arithmetic and logic unit
baud rate	bits per second
bit	binary digit
bps	bits per second
CAD	computer-aided design
CAL	computer-assisted learning
CAM	computer-aided manufacture
CNC	computer numerical control
COM	computer output on microfilm/microfiche
cps	characters per second
CPU	central processing unit
DAC	digital-to-analogue converter
DBMS	database management system
DDE	direct data entry
DPM	Data Processing Manager
EFT	electronic funds transfer
FAX	facsimile
G	giga
Gbytes	gigabytes (1 000 000 000 bytes)
IAS	immediate access store
IBG	interblock gap
JSP	Jackson Structured Programming
K	kilo
Kbyte	kilobyte (1000 bytes)
LAN	local area network
LSI	large-scale integration
MICR	magnetic ink character recognition
M	mega
Mbyte	megabyte (1 000 000 bytes)
modem	modulator/demodulator
OCR	optical character recognition
OMR	optical mark reader
PIN	personal identification number
RAM	random access memory
ROM	read only memory
VDU	visual display unit
WAN	wide area network

Index